JACK of CAPE GRIM

Dedication

To the Victorian and Tasmanian Aboriginal people and their fight for justice.

For Jill, Karina and Katie who put up with so much while I was writing this book.

JACK OF CAPE GRIM

A story of British invasion and Aboriginal resistance

By Janine Roberts

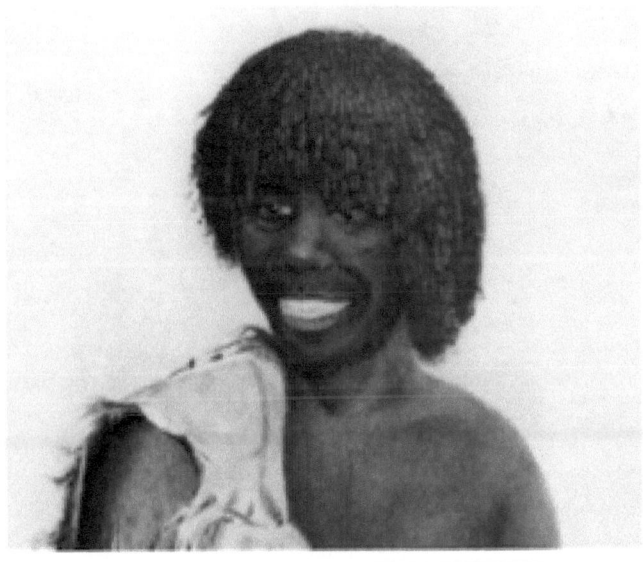

'Jack' of Cape Grim, NW Tasmania, Australia.

Published by IMPACT

First published in 1986 by Greenhouse Publications
Australia

Second Edition 2008
IMPACT Investigative Media Productions
Leonid
Bristol Marina
Hanover Place
Bristol BS1 6UH
UK
Email jackinfo@janineroberts.com
Web www.janineroberts.com/jackofcapegrim.html

© Janine Roberts 1986-2008

Cataloguing-in-Publication data:

    Roberts, J. P. F. (Janine Patricia Farrell)

    Jack of Cape Grim

    Bibliography.

    Includes Index.

    ISBN 978-0-9559177-0-7

1. Aborigines Tasmania – Government relations
2. Australia – History – 1834-1851
3. Indigenous races – Australia
4. History – Racism

Preface

I began to write this history in the middle of Melbourne's 150th year, in 1985, in reaction to the official ceremonies and events organised to mark that occasion. The 'triumphant' arch on Princes Bridge, all seemed to bear little relationship to the dramatic events that marked the first years in Melbourne.

The strangely neglected first hand-written records in this city, stored in cardboard boxes in a country warehouse, the letters home and confidential diaries of the first settlers, paint a picture of an unknown Melbourne, a centre for a private war between the younger sons of British aristocrats and the surrounding tribes.

Melbourne in 1839 was the strangest of settlements, a magnet for the ambitious younger sons of aristocracy, a haven for thousands of ocean-tossed sheep, a few rough-and-tumble wooden houses and tents on tribal lands in the remotest corner of the British Empire.

Hundreds of the inhabitants of this land gathered to watch the newcomers. For them it was as fascinating as a landing by Martians would be for us today, and perhaps as threatening. They camped across the river and on the outskirts, watching as the pallid-faced ones landed with thousands of sea-sick sheep and very few women, to plod their way up mud-tracks that passed for roads, drinking strange brews in the Melbourne Club – practically the only house of any size, toasting the stations they intended to carve out of tribal land, estates to rival those of any English lord for size.

These records tell of a Melbourne of aristocratic pretensions, built of huts and tents, where many a grandiose dream was born and built on a foundation of blood, the lives of the first Australians.

Buried deep in these records is the story of a most intrepid band of Tasmanians, three women and two men, who fought a startling campaign against the invading settlers on the Eastern outskirts of Melbourne, who had three military expeditions launched against them, whose exploits rival those of Ned Kelly and deserve to be at least as well known.

It is to their memory that I dedicate this book. I have had to write their story from the records of those they fought, but I have tried as far as I am able, to unravel the true events of their campaign, their final armed stand against the invaders.

Reviews

Jack of Cape Grim

'**Probing our Racial Injustice**' review by Guy Parsons. 'The book is an extensively researched account of five Tasmanian Aborigines who declared war on settlers on the outskirts of Melbourne in 1841. ... The story of Jack is dramatic ... well researched'.

The Age; '**Barbarous spectacles that Melbourne forgot**' review by Stephen Downes. 'The story of a 'natural leader of the Aborigines' based on a "treasure trove" of material – letters, journals and official records.'

'**Aborigines had no reprieve from hanging**' by Noel Shaw. 'There is not much we don't know about Truganini, that comely and diminutive Tasmanian. Historians have found delight in her. Most artists of the early colony painted her portrait. Less well known ... is that she and four other Tasmanians went on a lawless campaign that would rival Ned Kelly's... they took off to join their fellows who were at constant warfare with the white invaders.' 'Jan Roberts has written probably the fullest account of this.'

Other Works of Janine Roberts

Roberts also wrote: "***From Massacres of Mining: The Colonization of Aboriginal Australia,***" of which the eminent author Xavier Herbert wrote: 'She handles her history with a restraint that makes it a work deserving to be established as a classic in our history... The effect on myself was profound. I who thought I knew "all about it" was appalled ... it should be required reading.'

She edited and co-authored '***The Mapoon Books***,' about an Aboriginal community's fight for justice and, successfully, to regain their much loved hunting lands, reviewed by an eminent Australian historian, Humphrey McQueen, as 'the finest, best researched and through study to appear in the Whitlam era.'

She co-produced with Aboriginal spokesman Robert Brotho the AFI Best Documentary Nomination winning "*Munda Nyuringu*" film on the West Australian Gold Rush and Aborigines. 'What happened to the Aborigines was a microcosm of what happened all over Australia.' Her role in this was reviewed in The Age under the headline 'Irish eyes bring Australia's dispossessed into sharp focus.' She also initiated and researched the highly praised Granada TV documentary '*Strangers in their own land*' and the BBC/ABC documentary '*Sacred Land Rites,*' both on Aboriginal land rights.

In recent years she has also worked with Canadian First Nations and with Black South Africans, authoring the book '***Glitter and Greed: the secret world of the diamond cartel.***' The literary editor of *The Independent* in the UK reported that this 'enthralling', 'formidably well-researched' 'gripping book for once merits that tarnished plaudit, "brilliant" and added: 'One of the most damning exposes of a near-monopolistic industry to appear in years. The wonder is that it appeared at all.'

She also made an investigative film, shot in six continents called '***The Diamond Empire***' for the BBC, WGBH Boston and the ABC (Australia) on human rights and the diamond trade. US Congresswoman Cynthia McKinney invited her to testify and show this film at a Congressional Hearing and said: 'Janine Roberts is that rare individual who speaks truth to power ... I count myself among the privileged of this world to know Janine and her work.'

She has also written, under her family name of 'Farrell-Roberts,' an entertaining, thoughtful and honest memoire '*the Seven Days of my Creation*' that describes, among other things, how her life was enriched, and endangered, during the 15 years she spent working with Aborigines in the Outback and for other oppressed peoples. "Robust scholarship runs throughout this passionate and honest autobiography... Hers is a strong voice that both challenges and touches the heart.' 'Fascinating, and inspirational – and a must read.'

And about to appear – her investigation of the pharmaceutical industry '***Fear of the Invisible.***' This draws on inside-industry sources and paints a well documented picture of the appalling medical carelessness and poor science that today undermines the safety of vaccines and anti-viral medications, including those given against AIDS. This book developed out of a Channel 4 Dispatches program '*Monkey Business*' that she co-produced with Rosie Thomas.

Forward to the new Edition

Over the past few years I have been filled with dismay by how some historians have renewed the former Australian custom of whitewashing their early history, again denying it was one of invasion, skirmishes, battles and massacres. Thus I felt a need for a new edition of this book as it is based on the original handwritten accounts of people living in those days.

Did the Aboriginal people have heroes? Did they fight for their land like the Apaches and Sioux of North America? Yet, they did. The original records tell of how they fought – and were massacred, and how survivors were put in reservations. There were many heroes and heroines in this struggle. This book is about some of them.

Since this book was first published, the Aboriginal peoples have regained some of their lost rights. But in most of South-Eastern Australia and Tasmania they have only secured their rights to a few scattered islands and small areas, including where Truganini, Jack and other Aborigines were once held captive. But it should be said; in Tasmania by 2002 they only had their rights recognised to less than one hundredth of one percent of their former lands.

Just north of Cape Grim, the small Steep Head Island was restored to the ownership of Tasmanian Aborigines, and today it supplies some with a traditional food, the mutton-bird.

The shoreline at Cape Grim is still wild, with high cliffs, rock arches, sandy beaches and, just offshore, the Doughboy Islands remain wild where the women once hunted seals, with the men hunting up in the high-tufted grasslands and forest of the cliff tops.

Regretfully, when the Tasmanian Aborigines asked recently for the restoration of their rights to Cape Grim itself and to the close-by Doughboy islands, on the grounds of "their spiritual significance to Tasmanian Aborigines" and of the massacres recorded in this book, they were refused.

Instead this land is still held today by the sheep station company that originally threw off the Aborigines and whose original staff may have been responsible for the massacre of Jack's people recorded in this book. It is the Van Diemen Land Company and it arrived here in 1826. It boasts it holds the oldest Royal Charter – and that it still has its original 1830s jail.

On top of Cape Grim, near to where the bodies of Jack's relatives were thrown over the cliff, there now stands 'The Cape Grim Baseline Air Pollution Station' which monitors the atmosphere of the Southern hemisphere. One of the leading scientists here is on record for mistakenly saying that there is no Aboriginal claim to this Cape. Nearby a company bottles the exclusive up-market 'Cape Grim Water,' sold as the least polluted in the world.

But they make no mention of the people who long cared for this land and kept it pristine. These people did not let us drive them into extinction. They fought for and loved this land – and still love it. We honour the war dead of Gallipoli in memorials all over Australia. It is surely time to similarly honour the war dead of the Aborigines.

Jan Roberts   March 2008

Contents

1 The Tasmanians	1
2 Move the Tasmanians to Port Phillip	10
3 The Squatters	21
4 Melbourne Protected	39
5 Melbourne Aborigines Take Up the Gun	49
6 The Tasmanians Fight	61
7 The Trial	80
8 The Execution	90
9 The Sequel	95
Endnotes	108
Selected Bibliography	116
Index	118

Jack, Native of Cape Grim, Van Diemen's Land, Thomas Bock, watercolour on paper, Tasmanian Museum and Art Gallery

Robert, Native of Van Diemen's Land,
Thomas Bock, watercolour on paper,
Tasmanian Museum and Art Gallery

Fanny, Native of Van Diemen's Land,
Thomas Bock, watercolour on paper,
Tasmanian Museum and Art Gallery

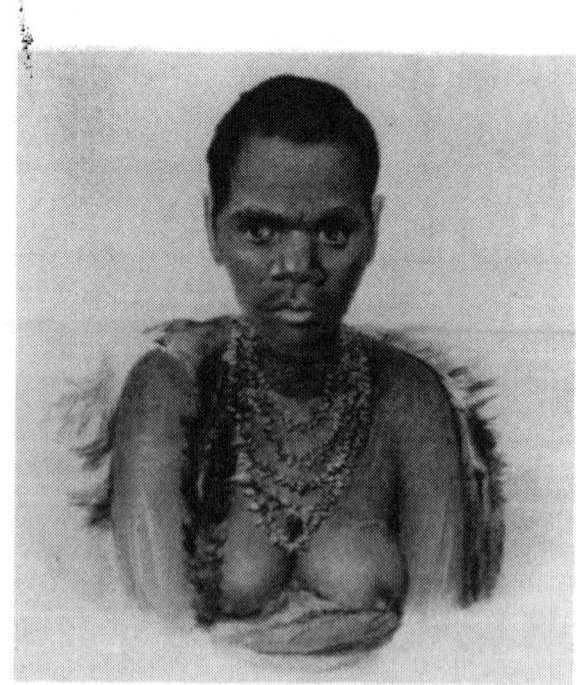

The Conciliation 1840, Benjamin Duterrau, oil on canvas, shows Truganini with Robinson during the rounding-up of the Tasmanian Aborigines. Woorraddy holds her left hand. *Tasmanian Museum and Art Gallery*

Truganini (Truggernana), Native of the Southern part of Van Diemen's Land, Thomas Bock, watercolour on paper, *Tasmanian Museum and Art Gallery*

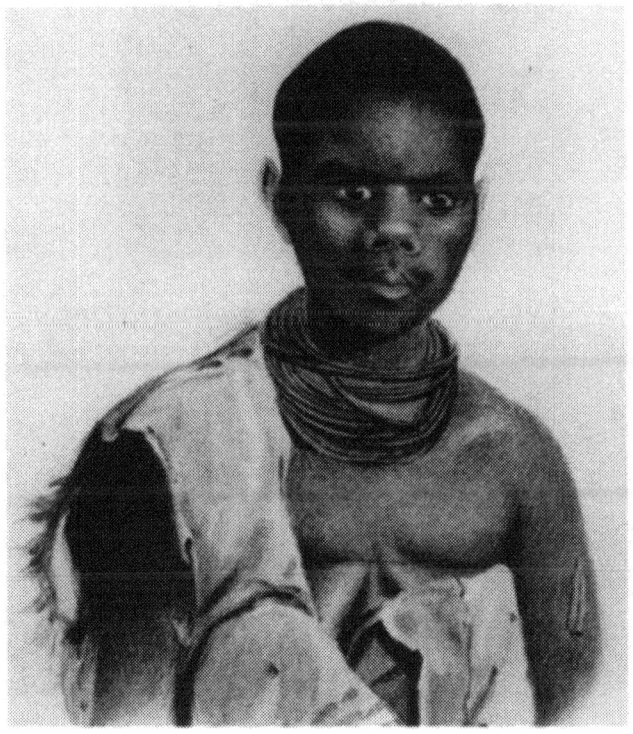

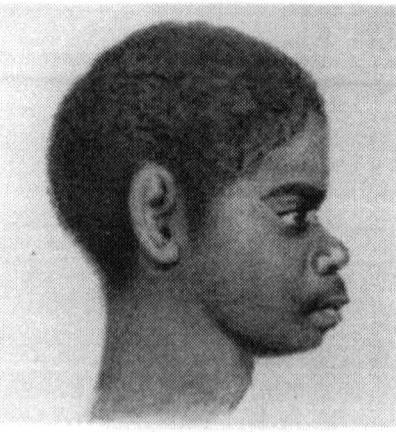

Truganini (Truggernana) 1834, Benjamin Duterrau, oil on canvas, *Tasmanian Museum and Art Gallery*

Truganini (Truggernana), Thomas Bock, monochrome on paper, *Tasmanian Museum and Art Gallery*

Chapter One
The Tasmanians

In 1841 a fever of excitement ran through a settlement of huts and tents called Melbourne, by a remote river in an alien and distant land. Many younger sons of English gentry were landing from tall ships docked in the river mouth; they were filled with plans for instant fortunes to be won from the sweeping grasslands and forests surrounding them, theirs for the taking. It was a time for instant estates, dwarfing those of earls and dukes, for optimism, land speculation and grandiose dreams.

Every day, when winds were favourable, tall ships would tack in through the Heads into the vast bay, carrying excited settlers and hopeful servants – together with horses, sheep, cattle, all the implements needed to fulfil their fantasies.

It was only six years since Melbourne had been founded, only five since it had become an official British settlement. Its population was now 8,000 strong. There seemed to be little that could hold it back. There now appeared to be no danger from the original inhabitants, especially in the nearby districts, although there were worrying reports of conflict from the border zones.

They were then horrified to read in the *Port Phillip Herald* on the morning of 29 October 1841 of an uprising just out of town.

THE BLACKS. Information has been received in town that numerous depredations have been committed in the Westernport direction by a party of Aborigines accompanied by and associated with two Van Diemen's Land blacks and three women who are as well skilled in the use of the firearms they possess as the males.

The daring party have extended their depredations to Dandenong and its vicinity, plundering Messrs Mundy's,

Westaway's and different other stations and committing unmentionable atrocities . . . possessing a large quantity of firearms.

Mr Thomas has been dispatched in pursuit in company with a strong detachment of the mounted police and a party of Aborigines. Another detachment of mounted police will leave town today under the command of the Commissioner, Mr Powlett.

They were appalled, too, at the re-appearance of their old foe, the Tasmanian Aborigines. Many of Melbourne's first citizens had just arrived from Tasmania. The Aborigines there had been defeated only after thirty-four years of bitter struggle, including, finally, three years of martial law under which troops were permitted to shoot Aborigines on sight.

By now this Aboriginal band had been raiding for many weeks. The latest account prompted a re-invigorated hunt, especially when the news came three days later that two white men had been killed. Mounted police, government administrators and army troopers were sent out on the chase while the owners of stations on the Mornington Peninsula either armed themselves to the teeth or fled back into Melbourne.

The panic was recorded in the beautifully inscribed letters of Henry Meyrick to his parents in England. Meyrick had been just one year in Australia. He was eighteen years of age and wrote, 'sitting on a sugar-bag and making a table of a flour-bag',[1] from Colourt Station on Westernport Bay near Sandy Point, on 25 November 1841.

> The whole neighbourhood has been thrown into the utmost confusion, as the newspapers would say, by three Van Diemen's Land blacks, who were brought over as servants by Robertson, the Chief Protector, and ran away, making common cause against all white men. They murdered four and robbed Allen's station which is ten miles from Colourt. Had they come on to Colourt we would have robbed the hangman of his fee for we had guns loaded enough to have annihilated a whole tribe.*

He was one of the brave. Government officials reported that the owners of many of the homesteads and stations had fled back to Melbourne.

---

* See Chapter 3 for a fuller record of Meyrick's fascinating correspondence.

Who were these desperadoes? There were not three as he imagined but five. Ironically they were a party of Tasmanian Aborigines brought over to Victoria by the Official Protector of Aborigines, Robinson, to 'civilize' the local Aborigines. He hoped to use them to persuade the local Aborigines to cease their fight against British settlement and to take up Christianity.

The *Port Phillip Herald* report continued: 'These people had been imported by Mr Robinson for the purpose of aiding in the civilization of the Aborigines of Australia Felix.'[2]

Among them there was the famous Truganini,[3] the so-called 'Last of the Tasmanians'. She, with her women friends, Matilda and Fanny, was reputed to be as good a shot with the gun as the men in the group. There were two men with them, Jack of Cape Grim and Robert of Ben Lomond. All of them had come to Victoria after witnessing the most horrific disaster befall their race.

They came from every quarter of Tasmania. Truganini came from the South-East tribe, Matilda from the rugged west coast. Fanny was Jack's wife. Her tribal name was Planobeena. Both Fanny and Matilda had been taken by sealers from their tribes. Bob came from the central hills near Ben Lomond, Fanny probably from the Tamar Valley below Ben Lomond.[4]

Cape Grim Jack was then about thirty years old. He bore the name Cape Grim after a rugged headland in his tribal lands of north-west Tasmania. Here, when he was fifteen years of age, shepherds had shot thirty Aborigines and flung their bodies over a thirty metre cliff in revenge for their killing of 118 sheep. They gave the cliff the name it still bears, Victory Hill.[5] He was born in 1812 on an island now called Robbins. His Aboriginal name was Tunnerminnerwait. By then European sealers had been seasonally hunting in north-west Tasmania for eight years. By the time he was thirteen the sealers had wiped out nearly the entire population of elephant seals and kangaroos on his island.

Tunnerminnerwait's people were part of the North-West tribe. They would travel every year along the coast from the north-west corner right down to Macquarie Harbour. All this was their land. They had well marked trails down the coast with permanent beehive-shaped huts at all the major seasonal hunting grounds. They dug and maintained wells, leaving shell drinking-cups for visitors.

They would go inland, too, with the permission of the Northern tribes, to mine ochre in the Surrey Hills. They would also travel down to visit the South-West tribe on the southern part of the west coast, crossing Macquarie Harbour in bark catamarans. They would go north for mutton birds and south for elephant seals at the assigned hunting times. They would go to coastal lagoons for eggs in spring.

When Jack was fourteen, the Tasmanian Land Company moved into the area, setting up sheep stations at Cape Grim and Circular Head. On 27 November the next year, 1827, an Aboriginal tribe visiting Cape Grim found there several shepherds, huts and many sheep. The shepherds tried to entice the Aboriginal women into their huts; the Aboriginal men objected and, in the resulting fight, one Aborigine was shot dead and one shepherd wounded.

It was then that the Aborigines, in revenge, drove a mob of sheep over the cliff on Victory Hill. Six weeks later the shepherds ambushed the Aborigines while they were mutton-birding, killing thirty people and throwing their bodies over the same cliff. After this, the Aboriginal people named the whites at Cape Grim the 'nowhummoe' or 'devils'.[6]

Disasters did not end there for the Cape Grim people. A month later they were ambushed by sealers who shot one man dead and abducted seven women to serve them in their camps on Kangaroo Island.[7] And another month later, a group of Aboriginal women swimming out after shellfish and mutton birds were ambushed by yet another group of sealers hidden in a cave when they swam back to shore. The men herded them at gun-point into a corner of a cliff, tied up all fourteen and took them off to Kangaroo Island.[8]

In general, Aboriginal men were shot at sight and the women seized to serve the needs of shepherds and sealers, many of whom took two Aboriginal women each.

Cape Grim Jack was captured by George Augustus Robinson two years later in 1830, by which time only sixty Aborigines were estimated to remain alive in the north-west out of an estimated 500 or more living there just three years earlier. Robinson was engaged in rounding up all the free tribes of Tasmania to send them to a place of apparent safety on an island off Tasmania's north coast. However, at this time the tribes of the north-west avoided him. The only Aborigines he met were in a sealers' camp. The sealers had with them six abducted women and one man, Cape Grim Jack.[9]

Robinson forced the sealers to give up the Aborigines by threatening them with legal action if they did not. He told them he knew they had shot the husbands when abducting the women. He persuaded the Aborigines to come along by promising them immediate safety and eventual return to tribal lands.[10]

However, Jack was to escape from Robinson within a few months. He met up with others from the same part and absconded with them. Later he was recaptured and sent to Robinson's island 'refuge'.

Robinson wrote to the colony's administrators telling them it was absolutely essential that he should be supported in removing the entire population of Aborigines from the north-west before they were exterminated by the shepherds and sealers.[11] He said this would also protect the lives of the colonists. He offered to remove the Aborigines from the mainland for £1000. His offer was accepted.[12]

His advice, in fact, was disastrous for the Aborigines of Western Tasmania. White settlement was only a temporary thing along much of that coast. Soon the pastoralists and sealers would be giving up on this area – much would remain a wilderness, and still does to this day. In 1828 Governor Arthur had divided Tasmania in two. The 'settled' areas of the centre and south-east were to be principally for whites; the west and part of the north were to be principally for Aborigines.[13] He actually returned the first Aborigines Robinson sent into captivity back to their tribal lands.

The Aboriginal tribes of the west might well have kept much of their lands – and their health – if it had not been for Robinson persuading Governor Arthur that the west was too dangerous for Aborigines and that they should be removed to an island sufficiently far from the coast to impede attempts to swim back to the mainland.

This was especially tragic for Matilda, another member of the Melbourne rebel band, whose tribal name was Pyterrunner. She came from Port Pirie in the centre of the west coast. She had been seized by sealers then taken from them by Robinson. She would have been allowed to return with the other Port Pirie and west-coast Aborigines if Arthur's original policy had been kept to. Robinson rounded up the rest of her people at gun-point on one of his last collecting trips.

Pyterrunner was to be a victim of Robinson's 'matrimonial strategy' in 1837. She had refused to get married, as had several other women, so Robinson organised 'marriages' for her and three others. He believed that once married they would settle down and be easier for him to manage! But within a week they ran away from their husbands and into the bush. They refused to return until Robinson agreed they could live as they chose. Robinson refused them rations, so they robbed the camp at night. Within weeks his efforts to get the Aborigines to live in nuclear families collapsed. They all went back to their own communal, traditional style of life.[14]

The authorities had other reasons to support Robinson's request. The northern tribes had started to arm themselves with guns to defend their lands. Two years earlier, just after the Cape Grim massacre, an Aboriginal woman escaped from the sealers and became the leader of Aboriginal people living around Emu Bay on the central northern coast. She taught them how to use guns captured from the settlers. Her name was Tarerenorerer; the sealers called her Walyer.[15]

Tarerenorerer was eventually recaptured by sealers in 1830. When she refused to serve them, two of them took her to a small island to keep her in isolation. She tried to kill them, so, when the sealers were contacted by Robinson, they were glad to give her up, though Robinson also found her hard to handle. She died of influenza within months of being sent to his 'refuge' island, like so many other inmates of his reformatory.

Two of the other three members of the Dandenong guerilla band came from inland Tasmanian tribes. Fanny, Jack's wife, probably came from the upper Tamar valley. Robert, also known as Peevay, came originally from Ben Lomond highlands, which were highly regarded by other tribes as a summer resort. They themselves had foraging rights on the north and east coasts and would winter near the sea.

The fifth member of the band, Trucannini, or Truganini, had been with Robinson from the start of his Aboriginal work in 1829 when she was just eighteen. He met with Truganini on Bruny Island. She was one of the nineteen survivors of the Southeast tribe which, six years earlier, numbered about 200. Her tribal land stretched from the southernmost part of Tasmania up to the Derwent River.

She was a very beautiful woman, slim and small, only about 4 ft 3 ins in height (129 cm). She was renowned for her beauty. Her portrait was to be painted by most of the artists in the colony. Like all Tasmanian women, she wore her hair short, unlike the men, who wore their hair in long, natural, tight curls, often stiffened with ochre.

Truganini was born in 1812 on Bruny Island in the D'Entrecasteaux Channel. She was one of the last of her people to be reared in their many thousand-year-old tradition for, just one year later, Hobart was founded by British authorities. Her people had greeted many explorers without hostility but by 1812 were beginning to suffer from the slave raids of the sealers, who stole women not just as concubines but also to act as slave hunters for the seal.

When she was still a child, Truganini's life was brutally interrupted when a party from a whale-boat burst into their camp stabbing her mother to death.[16] In 1828 another group of sealers abducted three of her tribal sisters. Her stepmother was seized by a group of mutinying convicts in 1829 and never seen again. As a teenager, Truganini took a boat with two Aboriginal men, including her husband-to-be, and two white men. On the way back to her island, the white men threw the Aboriginal men into the sea. When they tried to climb back into the boat, their hands were axed off. They were then left to drown as the two whites rowed Truganini off to rape her.[17]

During all these years there was no case reported of an Aborigine raping a white, and no white man was ever legally punished in Van Diemen's Land for killing an Aborigine.

Robinson arrived on Bruny Island a short time later. He was being paid by the government as part of a new strategy to use civilians to gather up Aborigines and remove them to official reserves, while at the same time using the military under martial law to force the tribes into leaving white-occupied parts of Van Diemen's Land.

Martial law was proclaimed in 1828 and was to remain in force until Robinson was appointed in 1829. He was initially paid £100 a year. Bruny Island was looked on as a safe place for him to start. The Executive Council had said all the tribes, 'except the tribes who visit Bruny Island, are activated with one common purpose of murdering the white inhabitants.'[18]

However, within one year, by 1830, there was only one surviving adult member of the Bruny people, Woorraddy. There were also five young people: Truganini, Woorraddy's two sons, Peter and Davy Bruny, and two other girls, Dray and Pagerly.

That year the government offered a £5 bounty for every adult Aborigine captured alive, and £2 for every child. Robinson set out on a long, arduous journey up the west coast to see if he could capture some and put them in his depleted mission. He took with him the Bruny Island people and others including Robert Smallboy, a lad from Cape Portland. The Bruny Island Aborigines were a vital part of his strategy. He would send them on ahead to track the tribes and to tell them he came in peace. It was only on his latter expeditions that his men were to go armed.

He believed that their only way forward was to adopt a European way of life and to become Christian. This was for him synonymous with becoming civilized. However, within a short time illness had forced most of the Aboriginal adults to leave his camp on Bruny Island. He had separated the children from the adults. But he was ambitious. He wanted to change the way of life of the entire Tasmanian Aboriginal people, to save them, Christianize them, civilize them.

He journeyed through all parts of Tasmania trying to persuade Aborigines that their only hope of safety was to come with him. He told of the Governor's plan to use the 'Black Line' of troops to force Aborigines out of settled areas. He travelled with his 'mission blacks', Aborigines whom he had persuaded to trust him. Truganini, Jack, Robert and Matilda were some of those who did the most to help him execute his plans. They helped persuade some of the major guerrilla bands to come to his Flinders Island settlement. For his success the government granted him over 1000 hectares of land, a salary increase to £240 per annum back-dated to his initial appointment, and an immediate £100 gratuity.

While travelling, it seems he had an affair with Truganini. He recorded this in his diary but, as he wrote about it in the local Aboriginal language, it was only discovered when these notes were recently deciphered.[19] On one occasion Truganini saved him from drowning when he was fleeing from some of the North-West tribe.

In August 1831 they brought in Umarrah and his group – he was the best known guerrilla fighter in the settled areas of Tasmania. On 15 October 1831 he set off with Robert, Jack, Truganini and others to find the Big River Tribe, which he captured on 31 December 1831. But during all these searches, he misled the Aborigines helping him by promising that as a reward they would be allowed to remain in their own lands. In fact, he believed that while they remained in their own country they would not become Christian. He showed no intention of letting Aborigines return to their lands once he had them on Flinders Island.

For capturing the Big River tribe he received an award of £100. The Aborigines who assisted him received a flock of fifty sheep. Robinson then negotiated a contract for £1000 if he were to completely clear the mainland of Aborigines by bringing in the west-coast people.

In 1832, Robinson and his mission blacks set out for a second long expedition along the west coast. This time the white men with him carried guns. He looked forward to success. 'By taking the whole [of the Aborigines] I gain not only the reward but the celebrity.'[20]

In 1835 he reported to the Colonial Secretary that 'the entire Aboriginal population are now removed' and claimed his reward.[21] There was at least one family he had overlooked, but now the settlers could freely go without their guns. The thirty-year war was over.

Robinson decided to rename 'his' Aborigines. The nick-names given to them by the settlers were often demeaning; their Aboriginal names were rarely used by whites. So he gave them all new names: Truganini became 'Lalla Rookh' after a fabulously beautiful Indian princess; Woorraddy became 'Count Alpha'; and Jack of Cape Grim, 'Napoleon.' He bestowed them with the new names at a banquet of roast swan, suckling pig, fish and potatoes.[22]

Despite such frivolities, Flinders Island was a disaster. Many Aborigines who had been in good health when captured, died soon after being sent to the prison island. The island was swept by deadly epidemics. By 1837, three-quarters of the Aborigines sent to the island had died.

Disillusionment with Robinson set in once the Aborigines realized he would not let them return to tribal lands and would not respect their traditional culture. They accused Robinson of neglect, openly defied his authority, wore ochre and performed ceremonial rites, refusing to behave as 'Christians'. The ones who took the lead in this were some of his trusted mission blacks: Jack, Fanny, Truganini, Bob and others, who were freshly returned from searches for the last of the Aborigines on tribal grounds.[23]

Chapter Two
Move the Tasmanians to Port Phillip

Robinson's ambitions stretched beyond Van Diemen's Land. He saw his Flinders Island establishment being transported to Port Phillip, the original 'white' name for much of what is now known as Victoria, and being rapidly expanded to cover all the Aborigines of that area, through new regional stations on which they could be civilized. Far from intending to take the Aborigines he had collected back to their homelands as he had promised, he planned to bring them all with him to the mainland of Australia. They would be at the core of the new settlements.

On 27 September 1835, before Batman set foot on the site of Melbourne, the Lieutenant Governor of Van Diemen's Land, Sir George Arthur, wrote to the Colonial Office to say:

> I have much pleasure in informing you that Mr Robinson has offered his services to take the Aborigines from Flinders Island to Portland Bay in the hope that he might, through them, open a friendly communication with the natives there.

He went on to say that the Tasmanian authorities would pay to support the surviving deported Tasmanian Aborigines. Thus, although this was not the stated purpose, Tasmania would finally be rid of all its original inhabitants. To ensure the success of this endeavour, Robinson offered to send a party of troops to Portland Bay with them, in case of conflict between them and local Aborigines! Robinson asked, about the feasibility of this plan, replied:

> If the mild and benevolent measures pursued by this Government towards the Aboriginal inhabitants of this island have proved so successful, how much easier will it be to effect a

reconciliation with a people less incensed? The system adopted towards the Aborigines of this territory is, I believe, quite unique; history does not furnish an instance where a whole nation has been removed by so mild and humane a policy.[1]

He stated that moving the Tasmanians to the mainland could save their lives, in that it would cure them of the diseases from which they were dying on Flinders Island. This, he said, was not a physical illness but rather 'mental irritation' caused by longing for their own tribal lands! The cure of returning them to their homelands was not considered. He explained his extraordinary theory thus:

By being far removed from their native land they would be less liable to mental irritation – although the deaths of the Aborigines at Flinders Island may be ascribed to other causes, as catarrh, inflammation, etc. Still it will be found that mental irritation accelerates, if not the disease, the suffering of the patient, and in too many instances has proved fatal.[2]

Finally they would be useful for:
1. Exciting curiosity in the minds of the New Hollanders.
2. Conveying supplies, they being more to be depended upon, than the Aborigines of that country.
3. People of colour and especially the Aborigines of Van Diemen's Land, are preferable to white men for this particular duty [of carrying supplies]: they can endure great privations. Their wants are sooner supplied, and they will seldom repine, when pressed with hunger or overcome with fatigue.[3]

This plan was strongly opposed by the authorities in Sydney although approved by the British authorities. Lord Glenelg wrote to Sir George Arthur on 3 August of that year saying they could not agree.

Sir Arthur, in his reply of 21 October 1835, explained some hitherto unmentioned reasons for the Tasmanian authorities' support of Robinson.

There can be no doubt that the value of the Crown property has been much augmented by the issue of the persevering exertions of Mr Robinson. It is one of the most influential causes of the present prosperity of the colony and of the high prices brought by the wastelands of the Crown when exposed for sale by public auction.[4]

In addition to Robinson himself being guaranteed 'a gratuity of £1000 as soon as he had captured the whole of the Aborigines',[5] his sons were given grants of land.[6]

Governor Arthur suggested in June 1837 that Robinson be offered £500 a year to work at Port Phillip and have assistant protectors to help him. He wrote on 22 July:

> Even in a pecuniary point of view, the Government will be amply repaid. From what has happened within the last four years in Van Diemen's Land, Your Lordship has the proof... for no sooner was that country relieved from the dreadful outrages of the Aborigines, and from the lawless conduct of the convicts, than land, almost suddenly, rose in value from 50-100 per cent *at least!*[7]

Sir Arthur said he regretted his earlier methods of dealing with Aborigines in Van Diemen's Land for they led to a vast loss of Aboriginal life. He thought that if Robinson's tactics could be followed in New Holland and the natives brought into Aboriginal stations, then 'an enormous sacrifice of human life' would be avoided.[8]

Sir Arthur was recommending Robinson for the new post of Protector, created through the pressure of the British Anti-Slavery Society. Their concern over the treatment of Australian Aborigines brought about an Inquiry by the House of Commons Select Committee on Aborigines. In its report of 1837 the Committee recommended the office of Protector be set up because of numerous reports of atrocities. It justified the expense thus:

> When it is remembered that unsettled land has been sold by the Government of New South Wales, yielding in a single year returns to the local Treasury exceeding £100,000, and that in the recollection of many living men every part of this territory was the undisputed property of the Aborigines, it is demanding little indeed on their behalf to require that no expenditure should be withheld which can be judiciously incurred for the maintenance of the missionaries, who should be employed to instruct the tribes, and of protectors, whose duty is should be to defend them.

Despite this concern, the Committee decided that there was no point now in talking about the justice of the seizure or of treaties with the tribes.

The new Governor of Van Diemen's Land, Sir John Franklin, was evidently as keen to see the Aborigines leave as Sir Arthur. In August 1838 he wrote that it should make life safer for Port Phillip settlers by mixing 'the domesticated blacks with the less civilized tribes'. He repeated the offer to pay for their upkeep at Port Phillip.[9]

He suggested taking with them the Flinders Island sheep, given to Truganini and the others who had helped Robinson round up their people, since it might excite in the mainland Aborigines 'the spirit of acquisition and consequent civilization'.[10] However the New South Wales authorities had the very opposite opinion.

A New South Wales Legislative Council Committee, under the Chairmanship of the Anglican Bishop of Australia, recommended strongly that the Van Diemen's Land Aborigines stay where they were. They said that to move them to Port Phillip would risk exposing their settlers

to acts of violence and rapacity on the part of the Aborigines similar to those by which the Colony of Van Diemen's Land was formerly devastated, and rendered almost untenable for the white population.

The natives now assembled at Flinders Island are the relics of the men by whom those ravages were perpetrated and there is but little doubt, may themselves have been personally engaged in acts of violence, rapine and murder. It is impossible to say that the seeds of the same evil disposition may not yet be lurking within their minds.[11]

The Committee feared they might excite the local Aborigines to 'the same fierce and hostile deportment towards the settlers.' They believed that 'the apparent civilization and improvement of disposition may be but delusive.'

'If it be real,' they added, 'they should then not be removed to the New Holland but with more propriety, restored to liberty in their native land.' Needless to say, the authorities ignored this latter recommendation.

Sir George Gipps reported: 'The project of removing these blacks to Port Phillip was no sooner known than it was met by the most decided opposition from all classes in the Colony, and even in the council, I could not find a single member who would look upon it favourably.'[12]

A note attached to this letter gave new light on Robinson's motives. According to James Stephen, who was Colonial Office secretary, Robinson's 'motive for removing them was not the hope of arresting this mortality [on Flinders Island], which he regarded as inevitable, but *rather the wish to throw a veil over an event which he thought it desirable to withdraw from the knowledge of mankind*',[13] this event being the extinction of the Tasmanian Aborigines.

However, because of Robinson's urgent pleas, he was permitted to bring 'only a small number [one family] of the Flinders Island blacks as his personal attendants.'[14] Gipps added that if he were successful, he might eventually be permitted to bring the others.

On 12 December 1838, it was announced that Robinson had been appointed Chief Protector of Aborigines at Port Phillip.[15] Robinson then set about selecting the Aborigines he would bring with him, setting the boundaries of 'one family' as wide as he dared. He at first told the Governor that he had brought eight, but later admitted that fourteen had come including two 'stowaways'.[16] When questioned over this, he replied that Aborigines decide family boundaries differently from us, and that he thought Governor Gipps meant by 'family', the family of natives that assisted him. Gipps had decidedly not meant this and informed Robinson he could only have rations for a family of *four*.[17]

The Colonial Secretary informed the Governor on 17 December 1839 that Robinson was to bill the Van Diemen's Land government for the rations,[18] and that if he did not provide sufficient information to satisfy that government, then the Aborigines would all have to be maintained at his own expense. It is uncertain just what support Robinson did receive.

Initially Robinson tried to use the Aborigines as he had planned. He introduced them to local Aborigines and tried to use them around Melbourne as he had in Van Diemen's Land. He reported:

> In the beginning of March, I arrived at Port Phillip and found the Aboriginal natives congregated in the environs of the township in considerable numbers. As as it was intended to employ the Van Diemen's Land natives as mediators and instructors to those people, I took an early opportunity of introducing them to each other. Their reception was of the utmost friendly character, and has continued so to the present moment.[19]

What they saw, he continued, was an Aboriginal people among whom 'disease, destitution and wretchedness prevailed to an alarming extent.' He recommended the immediate formation of an establishment similar to his on Flinders Island where they could be schooled and taught trades.

> Such an Establishment therefore should in my opinion be entered upon without delay, not only for the purposes proposed, but to afford an asylum to which the Aboriginal natives may, when their erratic dispositions permit, take refuge from the wide-spreading encroachments and cupidity of the squatters. I am not aware of the extent of land reserved for the Aboriginal natives, for excepting the grant on the south bank

of the Yarra River (since cancelled), I cannot learn that any other exists in the whole range of country mapped and sectioned off for the auctioneer's hammer. It would appear but an act of common justice that the tribes and remnant tribes should be permitted to select in their own districts small portions of land to be held by the Government for their use and behalf exclusively.

Such suggestions will naturally arise when it is known that many of the squatters, with their twenty and forty square miles of country, absurdly imagine that a £10 License to Squat confers on them the power to expel the primitive inhabitants from the land of their forefathers ... squatters would openly avow their sentiments, boasting that they never allowed an Aborigine to appear on their run, for the instant they were seen, mounted stockmen were sent with bullock whips to drive them away, and, I believe at the present juncture, there are still instances where lynch law, or violent expulsion, is resorted to. Nine-tenths of the outrages done by the Aborigines have been in just retaliation for wrongs committed against them by the whites.

Two years later Judge Willis was to maintain in the Port Phillip Supreme Court that the squatters were legally correct in expelling the Aborigines (see Chapter 7). Just three years earlier, when the Port Phillip settlement was less than one year old, visitors reported a very different picture.

The settlement is seldom without a few of them [Aborigines] – often 150 and 200 have been together. The Jaga Jaga tribe is said to be the most powerful of any. The men are generally fine, tall, well made fellows. The tribe is said to muster 450. They are very fond of flour – and other foods – but milk, spirits, wine or malt liquors they will not taste, a few have learnt to smoke.[20]

Another report in the same paper a month later verified their dislike of alcohol.

Yet before Europeans arrived in Melbourne, the tribes had suffered the most devastating of blows. It has recently been calculated that at the time the First Fleet reached Sydney in 1788, the Aboriginal population of what is now Victoria may have been 100,000.[21] By the time Batman arrived, the Aboriginal population in the Victorian region had dropped to about 15,000.

Like forest fires, plagues had raged across Australia. The First Fleet carried small-pox to Australia, an illness of which this continent was totally free. Its effect could only be compared to the horrific Black Death plagues of mediaeval Europe. A member of the First Fleet, Watkin Tench, described what he saw around Botany Bay just three months after they had arrived.

> An extraordinary calamity was now observed among the natives. Repeated accounts brought by our boats of finding the bodies of Indians [Aborigines] in all the coves and inlets of the harbour; pustules, similar to those occasioned by smallpox, were thickly spread on the bodies.[22]

William Bradley recorded at around the same time:

> From the great number of dead natives found in every part of the harbour, it appears that the small pox had made dreadful havock among them – scarce any Aborigines have been seen lately except lying dead.[23]

The plague did not stop at Sydney Harbour. It swept through south-east Australia in 1789. Other plagues followed: influenza, measles, syphillis – all literally decimating the Aboriginal tribes of Australia.

We know that the Victorian Aborigines once had permanent villages built of stone and other materials; we know that they fish-farmed on a large scale, building canals hundreds of metres long linking river systems with the sea, placing permanent weirs and fish traps across rivers, planting out yams as they dug up the new harvest. They used nets 100 feet by twenty feet, stretched across rivers to catch ducks. They would throw boomerangs high up over flocks in flight and, imitating the hawk's cry, force the birds down into the swiftly lifted net.[24] The first European settlers occasionally witnessed these hunting methods. But by then, Aborigines had much less need of such intensive hunting and proto-farming methods. By the time Melbourne was founded, a generation had passed since the first plagues. Many devastated Aboriginal communities would still have been trying to rebuild their lives .

George Langhorne, who preceded Robinson as a missionary and administrator with the Aborigines at the Port Phillip settlement, reported in 1836:

> In this year, the Aborigines' population in a circuit of, say, thirty miles around Melbourne numbered at least 700 men, women and children. They were divided into three tribes, the Waworong, the Bonurong and the Watowrong.[25]

The Waworong tribe inhabited the district extending from the Yarra River to Westernport. Jaga Jaga was reported to be a member of this tribe. The Watowrongs were around Geelong, and the Bonurong around Westernport Bay, according to Langhorne.

George Augustus Robinson c.1840, Benjamin Duterrau, oil on canvas, *Tasmanian Museum and Art Gallery*

Woorraddy (Woureddy), Native of Bruny Island Van Diemen's Land, Thomas Bock, watercolour on paper, *Tasmanian Museum and Art Gallery*

Woorraddy (Woureddy) 1834, Benjamin Duterrau, oil on canvas, *Tasmanian Museum and Art Gallery*

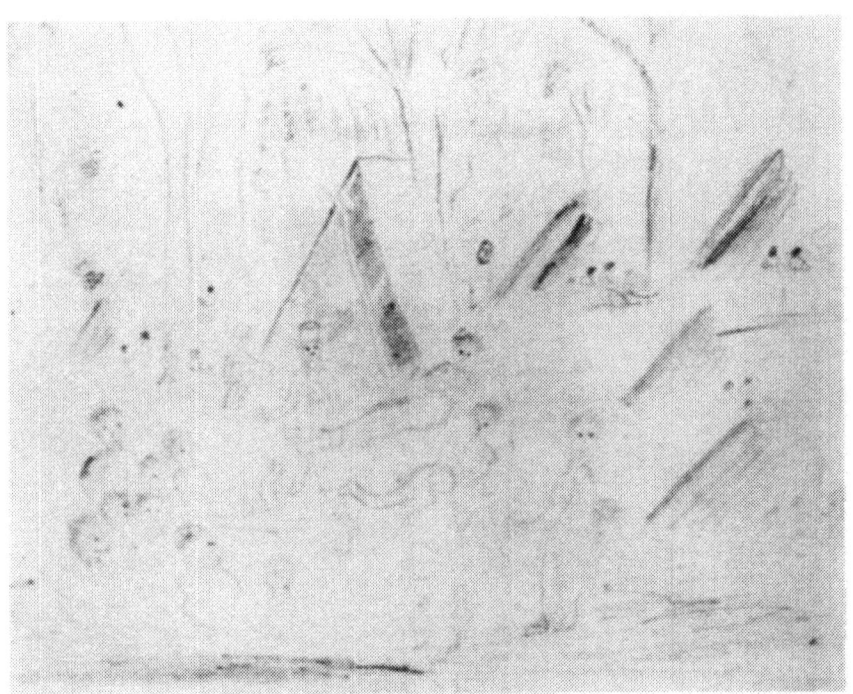

The Protector of Aborigines ('centre, wearing top hat) attempts to explain British law to a group of Aborigines 5 April 1843, *La Trobe Library*, State Library of Victoria

Tullamarine and Jin Jin set fire to the thatched roof of Melbourne's first gaol. W. F. Liardet watercolour, *La Trobe Library*, State Library of Victoria

Women and children of the Wurundjeri tribe 1858-9 (Victorians), Antoine Fauchery photograph, *La Trobe Collection, State Library of Victoria*

Men of the Wurundjeri tribe 1858-9 (Victorians), Antoine Fauchery photograph, *La Trobe Collection, State Library of Victoria*

Langhorne went on to recall the formal visit that year by the Governor, Sir Richard Bourke, to officially proclaim the settlement. He came in the ship *Rattlesnake* and set up his tent camp in what is now Collins Street.

The site of Melbourne at that time was very pleasing: the slope to the river intersected by the creek was covered with rich grass burned in the summer sun and scarcely as yet much-trodden by man or beast. Batman's Hill [down near the docks today], with its clumps of she-oaks, made a picturesque addition to the scene.[26]

There was a scattering of huts, made of wattle and daub (mud), and of tents. The Police Magistrate, Lonsdale, lived in two stockade huts built together, one a sitting room the other a bedroom, and behind other small huts for kitchen and servants' rooms. Of course there was a 'public house, partly weatherboard and partly canvas, the property of Mr J Fawkner.'[27]

When Europeans first arrived here, they were often welcomed as guests by the Aborigines. Initially many Aborigines thought that they were the spirits of dead relatives come back to visit them. How else could they explain these strange bleached individuals in their vast boats? William Buckley, a convict who escaped from Collins's original settlement on the Mornington Peninsula, had the good fortune to be recognized as the resurrected spirit of a leading Aboriginal elder because he was carrying a broken spear he had found marking that elder's grave. He lived with the Aborigines for thirty years before Melbourne's foundation and was treated with every respect.[28]

Dead relatives you do not greet with spears and clubs, so peace reigned initially in many parts. However, by the time Melbourne was founded, sealers and whalers had destroyed Aboriginal illusions and taught the power of firearms.

Conflict between Europeans and Aborigines did not take long to start. One of the first instances was reported on 15 March 1836 by a Mr Wedge,[29] when a party of Portland whalers had killed an Aboriginal mother and three children of the Westernport tribe.

Reports of killings escalated and Sir Richard Bourke made a formal effort to prevent it by proclaiming, on 3 May 1836, that British law extended westwards from Wilsons Promontory and that, under this law, all who injured Aborigines would be punished.[30] The Aborigines, too, were expected to obey this foreign dictate. As we will see, British law in fact was applied nearly exclusively to punish Aborigines. No whites were sentenced for killing Aborigines at Port Phillip for over ten years.

For example, when Governor Arthur, on 18 August 1836, reported 'there was no doubt that ten of the tribe of Port Phillip were killed' in revenge for the killing of two whites,[31] no legal action was taken because Aboriginal evidence was not acceptable to the courts.

Aboriginal resistance to the invasion often took the form of stealing potato crops or sheep rather than killing whites. This was done for reasons of survival because their own bush foods had been destroyed and because they wished to prevent the settlers remaining on tribal lands. Open conflict was more common away from Melbourne, in areas where the Aborigines were not so outnumbered.

Two Aborigines were arrested for stealing potatoes in what is now South Yarra. One of these was Tullamarine (who had Melbourne's international airport named after him), the other, Jin Jin. However, they escaped by setting fire to the reed roof of the gaol! The story goes that while the gaolers were asleep in the next room, Tullamarine broke a reed off the roof and poked it through the spy-hole in the door to get a flame from the lantern. They set fire to the roof and yelled for help. The gaolers woke and raced off to the barracks to get help. When they got back, the gaol-house was burnt down and the Aborigines gone.[32]

The following year, mounted police seeking Aborigines who had stolen sheep, 'captured half a dozen black women and brought them to Melbourne in the hope that the men who had fled to the bush would be induced to return to the outskirts of town through anxiety for their wives and daughters, and be an easy conquest.' The women were locked into the temporary Supreme Court, but during the night they removed some bricks from a wall and escaped.[33] This incident occurred in the same year as Robinson and the Van Diemen's Land natives arrived.

The conflict was most serious in the bush as the sheep stations spread out over the tribal lands. There were particularly heavy attacks along the overland routes to Port Phillip from Sydney. In 1838, 150 Aborigines attacked an overland party belonging to the Faithfulls near Benalla. About seven of the convict servants were slain and many sheep driven off.[34] The Faithfull brothers left their run as a result as did many others.[35]

There was only one case of white people being punished for killing blacks – the notorious Myall Creek Massacre north of Sydney. There, in June 1938, twenty-eight Aborigines, mostly women and children, were captured, tied up and hacked to pieces with swords and their bodies partly burnt. The seven shepherds responsible came to trial and were acquitted after fifteen minutes' deliberation by the jury. One of the jury told the press, 'I look on the blacks as a set of monkeys and the earlier they are exterminated from the face of the earth the better . . . I know well they were guilty of murder, but I for one would never see a white man suffer for shooting a black.'[36]

However their acquittal flew so much against the evidence that the authorities could not let it stand. They ordered a retrial. The shepherds were found guilty and hanged.

This remained a unique case of justice. From that day on the settlers made sure that their crimes against Aborigines were done away from official eyes and bodies fully burnt.

William Thomas, Assistant Protector to Robinson, reported that 'Since the executions in Sydney, settlers were more intent than ever on destroying the blacks.'[37] He said poisoning was widespread. Aborigines on many stations would take no milk or bread 'for fear it was poisoned'. Mercury and arsenic preparations used for sheep dressing were mixed with flour and baked.

Sir George Gipps summed up the attacks that had come to his notice in the first half of 1838 in a dispatch to Lord Glenelg in London on 21 July 1838:

1. Between the Rivers Ovens and Goulburn, a large convoy of sheep and cattle belonging to Mr W Pitt Faithfull, and under the charge of fifteen white men, was attacked by a party of blacks, said to have been 300 strong. Seven of the white men were killed, and the rest, as well as the whole of the cattle, dispersed in all directions. This occurrence took place about 400 miles from Sydney, and 150 from Port Phillip.
2. On 15 April the cattle station of Mr Samuel Jackson, near Port Phillip, was attacked by about fifty blacks, some of whom had firearms; about fifty sheep were carried away . . .
3. On 22 April Mr John Gardiner's station near Port Phillip was attacked by a party of blacks, some of whom had firearms.
4. On or about the same day a flock of 520 sheep . . . was driven away. All were recovered with the exception of forty-five.
5. On 6 May, the flocks of Dr Jonathan Clerke were attacked by a party of blacks, who had dogs with them, and twenty sheep were carried off.

6. On 19 May, Thomas Jones . . . was murdered by the blacks about sixty miles from Port Phillip.
7. On or about 22 May *all* the stations on the Barwon creeks, extending to a distance of more than thirty miles from Geelong were attacked, for the second time, by a party of about sixty blacks. Several huts were plundered. . . .
8. June 1. A black man . . . was drowned in an attempt to escape the persons in pursuit of him near Geelong. [He was chained and its weight dragged him down.]
9. June 9. Seven or eight blacks killed in defending a flock of sheep which they had carried away from the station of Mr Yaldwyn, about eighty miles from Port Phillip. On this occasion the blacks are said to have defended themselves with great bravery.

Because of Aboriginal resistance, Sydney settlers petitioned the colony's government and the British authorities on 8 June 1838, requesting the government to 'repress the tribes', who, they said, 'entirely without any provocation', were attacking the settlers, the 'pioneers of civilization', causing many to abandon their stations. The Melbourne to Sydney road could not be travelled without 'imminent danger to life and property'.[38] They feared they would not be able to take advantage of the 'new' lands near Port Phillip unless the tribes were suppressed.

In reply the Colonial Secretary on 12 August 1839 refused to levy war against the tribes, but took other measures.[39] He gave the Port Phillip authorities the power to send infantry into the interior against the tribes. Twenty-one mounted police were stationed at the Ovens River crossing and other garrisons were placed at intervals along the road. (Most of these developed into present-day townships on the Hume Highway.)

Chapter Three
The Squatters

The official record was only half the story. Obviously every attack by an Aborigine on a European was reported to the authorities, and a few extra concocted by settlers to excuse their actions, but it did not serve the purposes of many settlers to report attacks on Aborigines. However, sometimes they did write of them in their letters home or their private diaries.

There was great caution in the air because the strength of the Anti-Slavery Society in England was greatly feared. The Society had already helped bring about the hanging of seven shepherds for killing blacks at Myall Creek. It had forced Protectors on the colony at the settlers' expense. Many of the settlers saw these official British policies as totally unrealistic, if not just plain stupid. How could Aboriginal land be seized against Aboriginal resistance and Aborigines protected all at the same time?

Some of the finest private unpublished records from that time are the letters of Henry Meyrick, an English settler who arrived out here in 1840 and went to find himself a station east of Melbourne near Westernport Bay.[1] Another equally fine record is the journal of Niel Black, for the private use of friends who were thinking of joining him in Australia.[2]

It is only by going to sources like these that it is possible today to see just what were the concerns of the settlers in this infant British colony.

Niel Black sailed from the Clyde in Scotland on 11 April 1839, arriving in Sydney on 30 September after five months at sea and a brief stop-over in South Australia.

He was not long in Sydney, but did not find much there in accord with his low-church Scottish values. One night he went to the theatre:

> I never in my life before had an opportunity of seeing so numerous and such bulky samples of gaudy vulgar show – labouring under a load of fat and finery – as I had this evening among the dashing wives of Sydney.

He reported with some distaste that

> the great aim of life [here] is money; none come here but convicted rogues and those whose object is determinedly to pursue it. Therefore the most successful is the cleverest and most respected man.
>
> I believe this is not a place for Girls (generally speaking) making what is called good matches. There are just two things that occupy every young man's head here, that is Money and Home.

Home invariably referred to England.

However, as a lowland Scot he found in favour of convicts. 'It is the universal opinion here that a convict is a much preferable servant to a highlander.'

He came down to Melbourne by ship. This trip took three times as long as it should, for, when they got to the heads guarding the narrow entrance into Port Phillip Bay, a storm sprang up and kept them out at sea for six days more. When they eventually made their way between the Heads they ran aground immediately on a sandbank. It was another day before they could winch themselves clear and travel the short distance to the anchorage at Hobson's Bay.

Melbourne, then only four years old, impressed him greatly:

> Melbourne is, in my estimation, infinitely Superior to every other part of the Colony I have seen. The vaunted Morality and good society of South Australia sinks low indeed in the eyes of anyone who has had the opportunity of contrasting the quiet composure and content that sits on every countenance here – dressed in their best and moving along the streets to the different churches to which they belong.

It was clear why he liked the place, at least at first sight. 'Melbourne is almost altogether a Scotch settlement and the people are, as far as I can judge, altogether Scotch in their habits and manners.'

On 1 December his servants arrived from Scotland. He recorded the average wage for a shepherd was £25-£40 a year with full board. The average for a female servant was £15-£25. He was amazed to find that it was a society entirely run on bills of credit given against hoped for wool sales. People would buy and sell their stock on credit alone, with no money needing to change hands for three years or more. The squatters lived in the hope and expectation of future wealth.

Most of the squatters were the sons of gentry, for it took a £1000 or more to establish a station and that was a great fortune in those days. Black wrote, 'It is a rare chance to meet a person in the bush who is not a gentleman's son, or at least had a good education.'

A good but small starting off flock could comprise of 650 ewes at £1/3s each, fifty rams and wethers at £1 each and six bullocks at £20 each. This alone would total over £900. Very few labourers would ever save enough to start a flock.[3]

It was a rich man's frontier. One hundred and fifty-two 'gentlemen' squatters are recorded as coming to Port Phillip before 1850. One-third of them left again within this time as it was not as easy to start an outback station as they had imagined. Twenty-two of them died young. With the upper middle classes to swell the number, a total of 481 pastoral runs were authorized by 1840.

Since younger sons of the aristocracy and the upper middle classes rarely would have more than £1000 or £2000 as initial capital, they had little to spend on other things once they had purchased their stock.

Black recorded how most of them lived in the bush:
Many of the squatters have miserable huts and take a detestable pride in what they call roughing it. Their houses are made of split slabs thatched with bark. They eat damper and drink tea three times a day . . . They have no furniture even of the rudest kind, no windows to their huts.

They were almost entirely men – very few women came at first. The government made efforts to improve this situation by offering assisted passages for servants but only if equal numbers of each sex were brought out. By 1846, when Melbourne was 11 years old, matters had greatly improved. In that year there were four white men to every white woman.

Since the more stock the settlers had, the larger area they could claim for a run, most of those who had money on arrival would put nearly all of it into purchasing stock. They would then drive out their sheep and cattle to occupy as large an area as possible. Often they left themselves penniless in the process, hoping the size of their run would ensure them wealth in the years to come. Aborigines were only a hindrance to be disregarded and disposed of for such ambitious men.

Black recorded with scorn the 'pathetic remark' of a Mr Riddle who rode with him to view some country: 'Good God! What would the narrow-minded people of England say if they saw this scene when they talk so much of the Marquis of Hastings' paltry parke of 500 acres extent?'[4]

Those who settled in Melbourne also had their grandiose dreams. They saw themselves as the future leading citizens of a thriving city. Plans were quickly drawn for wide streets and civic buildings; construction was swiftly underway.

The gentlemen squatters wanted to recreate in Melbourne the genteel life to which they had been accustomed in England. The Melbourne Club, the Turf Club and three newspapers were all founded in those first years when Melbourne was little more than a collection of huts and mud roads.

Black wrote on 11 January 1840: 'I have heard it said that a child was drowned in the principal street [Collins Street] by the quantity of water that lay on part of it', and that one of the papers had, tongue-in-cheek, advertised government tenders for a punt to cross Collins Street!

Niel Black ran foul of the civic authorities on his first days in Melbourne when he was fined £1/2s/6d for having two unlicensed dogs! The day after he appeared in court, 3 December 1839, he set out alone to ride west from Melbourne for 100 miles to find himself a likely place for his station.

> I set out in good spirits and well hills in the far distance which appeared 'richly covered' with forest. That night I stayed in a shack that passed as an hotel.

He travelled on for days over extensive grassy plains sparsely interspersed with wind-blown trees, the only shelter incised rocky valleys and the occasional shepherd's hut.

He found all the sheep runs nearest to settlements were of a smaller size and mostly taken up. For the first time he became aware of the Aborigines whose land he had to take if he were to get a station. On 9 December he wrote:

> The best way [to get ahead] is to go outside [already settled areas] and take up a new run, provided that the conscience is sufficiently seared to enable him without remorse to slaughter natives right and left. It is universally and distinctly understood that the chances are very small of a person taking up a new run being able to maintain possession without having recourse to such means.
>
> Killing the Aborigines seems to be little thought of here as it is only defence of self or property. Two-thirds of them do not

1302 & 90d. The Blacks are very quiet here
now, poor wretches. No wild beast of the forest was
ever hunted down with such unsparing perseverance
as they are; men, women, and children are shot whenever they can be met with. Some excuse might be found
for shooting the men by those who are daily being
getting their cattle speared, but what they can urge
in their excuse who shoot the women and children
I cannot conceive. I have protested against it at every
station I have been in in Gipps' in the strongest language, but these things are kept very secret as the
penalty would certainly be hanging. Maurice was out
with a party after the blacks, but refused to fire on
them (as did another of the party, Young) to the intense indignation of the rest of the party, who returned leaving them unmolested. For myself if I
caught a black actually killing my sheep I would
shoot him with as little remorse as I would a
wild dog, but no consideration on earth would induce
me to ride into a camp and fire on them indiscriminately
as is the custom here whenever the smoke is seen. They
will very shortly be extinct. It is impossible to say how
many have been shot, but I am convinced that not less
than 450 have been murdered altogether. I remember
the time when my blood would have run cold at the
bare mention of these things, but now I am become so
familiarised with scenes of horror from hearing

Extracts from a letter from Henry Meyrick to
his family in England, Henry Meyrick papers,
La Trobe Collection, State Library of Victoria

Aborigines' encampment on the banks of the Yarra c.1842, J. Cotton, watercolour, *La Trobe Library, State Library of Victoria*

William Thomas, Assistant Protector of Aborigines, 1842, G. H. Hayden, pencil sketch, *La Trobe Collection, State Library of Victoria*

Port Phillip Aborigine fires a flintlock gun, *La Trobe Collection, State Library of Victoria*

Number 63.  [837]

SUPPLEMENT
TO THE
NEW SOUTH WALES
GOVERNMENT GAZETTE,
OF WEDNESDAY, AUGUST 26, 1840.

Published by Authority.

SATURDAY, AUGUST 29, 1840.

ANNO QUARTO.
VICTORIÆ REGINÆ.
No. 8.

By His Excellency Sir George Gipps, Knight, Captain-General, and Governor-in-Chief, of the Territory of New South Wales, and its Dependencies, and Vice-Admiral of the same, with the advice of the Legislative Council.

An Act to prohibit the Aboriginal Natives of New South Wales from having Fire Arms or Ammunition in their possession without the permission of a Magistrate.

Preamble. WHEREAS in some parts of the Colony of New South Wales the Aboriginal Natives have obtained possession of Fire Arms, and it is considered dangerous to the Public Security to allow the said Aboriginal Natives to have, keep, or use any description of Fire Arms or Ammunition, except as hereinafter excepted: Be it therefore enacted by His Excellency the Governor of New South Wales, with the advice of the Legislative Council thereof, That from and after the passing of this Act, it shall not be lawful for any Aboriginal Native, or Half-Caste usually abiding with such Natives, to have, or keep, any kind of Fire Arms or Ammunition, unless with the written permission of any Justice of the Peace resident in the district, which any such Aboriginal Native or Half-Caste shall usually frequent.

No Aboriginal Native or Half-Caste usually abiding with such Natives to have or keep any description of Fire Arms.

(Any Constable or Free Person may obtain or take from any such Native or Half-Caste any Fire Arms which he may have; provided no unnecessary violence be used.)

II. And be it enacted, That it shall and may be lawful for any Constable within the said Colony, or any Free person whatsoever, to obtain or take from any such Aboriginal Native or Half-Caste not holding such permission as aforesaid, every kind of Fire Arms or Ammunition which any such person may have, and lodge the same with the Police Magistrate of the District in which such Fire Arms or Ammunition shall be so obtained or taken; Provided, that no personal violence be used towards any such Aboriginal Native or Half-Caste, further than may be absolutely necessary for obtaining or taking such Fire Arms or Ammunition as aforesaid.

(Penalty on persons lending Fire Arms to any Aboriginal Native or Half-Caste usually abiding with such natives.)

III. And be it enacted, That it shall not be lawful for any person to give or lend to any Aboriginal Native, or any Half-Caste usually abiding with such Natives, not holding such permission as aforesaid, any Gun, Musket, Pistol, or any kind of Fire Arms or Ammunition whatsoever, and if any person whosoever shall give or lend to any Aboriginal Native or Half-Caste not holding such permission as aforesaid, any Gun, Musket, Pistol, or any kind of Fire Arms or Ammunition whatsoever, he or she shall, for every such offence, forfeit and pay a penalty of not less than ten pounds nor more than twenty-five pounds, to be recovered before any one or more Justice or Justices of the Peace for the said Colony.

(Recovery and Appropriation of fines.)

IV. And be it enacted, That all fines to be recovered under this Act, shall be proceeded for and levied in the manner provided by an Act of the Governor and Legislative Council of the said Colony, passed in the fifth year of the Reign of His late Majesty King William the Fourth, intituled " *An Act to regulate Summary proceedings before Justices of the Peace,*" and shall be paid to the use of Her Majesty, Her Heirs and Successors, for the Public uses of the said Colony, and in support of the Government thereof.

Proclamation to prohibit Aborigines from possessing firearms, 26 August 1840, *Victorian Government Printing Office and Public Record Office of Victoria*

care a single straw about taking the life of a native providing they are not taken up by the Protectors.

There is nothing but 'bouncing' [bragging] as it is called here and many persons bounce about their treatment of the natives. This they can only do by hints and slang phrases as the Protector of Aborigines is always on the lookout for information against the whites.

On Christmas Day 1839, sheltering in a shepherd's hut just after leaving Melbourne, he wrote:

> The poor creatures are slaughtered in great numbers and never a word said about it . . . When a new run is first settled, they steal the sheep and I believe they cannot easily be checked 'til a few of them are shot, being thus effectively frightened at first, they are easily kept down afterwards by threats until they become civilized.

It was a common Aboriginal tactic, and a very soundly thought out one, to make their primary target the sheep. If they destroyed a flock, they could effectively force the squatter to leave their land, for he could often not afford to purchase more. They would also dig up potatoes and destroy gardens to further sabotage the efforts of the settlers. In turn, this gave the Aborigines some redress, for much of their traditional plant foods were eaten by the flocks and their game was driven off. Because of the effectiveness of this tactic, the squatters would take bloody revenge on any Aborigine who killed sheep, sometimes wiping out whole tribes for the sake of sheep. Black wrote:

> The natives who have not been brought into subjection have a stong propensity to spearing and stealing sheep and cattle, and the settlers agree that lead is the only antidote that effectively cures them of this propensity.
>
> But this need not deter anyone from coming here as they may buy a run already occupied, and where the natives occasion as little annoyance, and I may with truth add much less, than a party of three or four tinkers of Gypsies do at home.
>
> Of this I am certain – a person bringing a set of decent men and women with him from home, who would behave as they ought, might live in perfect safety in the middle of the natives. They have no desire to take the white man's blood.

This was his first optimistic reaction. But the more experience he gained, the more he himself came to fear the presence of Aborigines and to realize that, come what may, he himself was living on a frontier and seeking to take and hold Aboriginal land against the wishes of the Aborigines.

He wrote on 18 January 1840:

> The Blacks, or natives, have occasioned me much uneasiness for some time. I could not stand the thought of murdering them, and to tell the truth, I believe it impossible to take up a new run without doing so, at least the chances are fifty to one. But after they have got the first taming by means of a few doses of lead effectively administered, it seldom happens they occasion much trouble after.

Eventually, on the far side of the plains, Black found the country he was looking for. He wrote enthusiastically of its beauty. It was, it seems from his description, in the borders of the Otway Ranges on the way to Portland.

He found there a station that met his requirement of having already 'tamed' its Aboriginal population. It was Strathdownie, which he renamed 'Glenormiston'. The previous owner, a Mr Taylor, had deserted the station for fear of the revenge of the local Jacoort tribe and of prosecution by the Protector of Aborigines.

> It is the opinion of Blacking [the former overseer], that about thirty-five to forty natives have been dispatched on this establishment and that there are only two men left alive of the tribe. He is certain we will never be troubled again with any of them on this run. I think myself remarkably fortunate in this run as well as upon this account as being perhaps, all in all, the best in the colony.

However, although Black was not attacked by Aborigines, they were still present. On his way to take up his run, he wrote on Sunday 9 February that he 'rode across bleak, barren and inhospitable plains.' [They were not barren to the Aborigines.]

> On one of the plains we spied five lubras [Aboriginal women] gathering roots. We were rather close upon them before they observed us, but when they saw us they fled with the swiftness of a roe. We gave them chase and came up with them. No creatures could be under greater fear than they were when they could not escape from us. The more we cried to them, the faster they fled, but all in vain. Such a cackling as they set up when we pulled our horses before them... One of them pulled a little female child out of a bag and presented us with it. We gave it a little damper and came away.

A staple of the Aboriginal diet was the mirr-n'yong root. The Aborigines bitterly complained of the sheep and cattle eating it up. 'Too many jumbuck [sheep] and bulgana [bullocks]. Plenty eat murnong – all gone murnong.'[5] One of the extremely rare white-women settlers, Mrs Katherine Kirkland, cultivated these roots as a vegetable in her garden. Most ignored them and instead planted potatoes. She also put her baby 'in a basket and hung him at my side as I had seen the native women do.'[6]

Black had only been two weeks at the station when the Protector of Aborigines called in to see him. Black was immediately apprehensive that Aborigines might follow the Protector about. Late that night the dogs started barking furiously.

> Donald Black and I got up, never doubting some of the natives followed the Protector and were about to steal our sheep. We each took a pistol which happened to be lying loaded in my room. We did not venture forth thus armed; we thought it prudent to go to the storehouse for our guns, and boldly sallied forth. All of a sudden we heard a rushing behind the garden. Donald ran as fast as his lame leg could carry him – and, had he got within sight of any object in the shape of a man . . .

Niel Black fortunately called out and was answered by his overseer, who was busy rounding up some escaped horses! Donald 'seemed astonished at himself and said that . . . if a black fellow had met him he would have done what till then he did not think himself capable of.'

Two days later, on 25 February, Black went out on horseback and met up with Aborigines who let him know what they wanted him to do. Some were, despite what he had been told, still living on the land he wanted to claim as a run.

> Rode out about four miles in search of springs for forming a cattle station. Saw some reeds and tea-tree, the invariable sign of good water in this district. Tea-tree springs are almost equal to the water at home. When closing upon the tea-tree, I saw three natives closely watching something in a tree. I was close upon them but they did not observe me, so intent were they on the game they were watching. At last I began to whistle carelessly to warn them of my approach.
>
> They all soon took up their spears and scampered off to the tea-tree. I followed, but they showed face when they got there. There was about twelve of them and they made a tremendous noise and yelling. One of them poised and quivered his spear although it was impossible for him to throw it more than half the distance between us.
>
> I walked my horse twice up and down past them, and when I turned away, they shouted and cheered and tossed their weapons in the air and cried "Grego mago" [Go away] . . .

> When at a short distance from them, I fired off two pistols and a gun to show them I had the power of injuring them severely if I chose to do it.
>
> When I returned the Protector was at my house. He is the most unpopular man that ever breathed. I have not yet formed any decided opinion of my own respecting him.'

Next day the Protector, probably Sievwright, left to go to Portland to investigate a case where five natives have been killed by whites.

Waterholes were extremely important traditional camping grounds for the Aborigines. They were also valued by the whites and were one of the first places the Aborigines were driven from. Next day Black set out to take over another popular Aboriginal water supply and camping ground, a lake he'd seen nearby.

> February 28th. Men dressing sheep. Sent out Anderson to set fire to the bush about the lake to prevent any person squatting on it for some time. I have a finer cattle run within one and a half miles of the home station, but by taking up the lake, I can claim all the country between here and there.
>
> The Blacks are numerous upon the banks of the lake, but they do not kill cattle and a horse is their terror if backed up by a man.

He did not consider in his diary the effect of burning the bush on Aborigines who happened to be there.

Next day he was busy glazing his windows. His house would be the second glazed house in the whole district. He had one sitting room, two bedrooms and fine verandah. He was fortunate in taking over such a fine house. The previous owner, Mr Taylor, fled before he had finished plastering it. It had wattle and daub walls and a thick, thatched roof. Black was thrilled with the land he was claiming.

> This is the most princely place I ever saw. I am delighted every time I ride round it. No Duke in Great Britain has a finer place. I claim ten miles square of the finest land in Australia and if I take possession of the lake, I will have much more.

He concluded, 'This I must do in a few days as others are on their way to put stock on.' On the evening of 6 March, more Scottish settlers arrived with a herd of cattle. They had introductions to him from people in Scotland but they were very cagey with him, refusing to say where they were going to settle except in vague terms. However, Black understood they were heading for the lake. So, at first light, he sent men out to race up to the lake with sheep to get there first.

He then warned the newcomers that he was already settled at the lake. They said vaguely that they were thinking of going down to the creek. So Black sent an urgent message up to the men at the lake asking them to divide the sheep and send some down to the creek too. 'We had five mounted men watching them and trying to guard every part.' They went up to the lake, and Black quickly rushed hurdles up after them to get his pen erected.

Black wrote in his diary, 'Possession is the first part in law here', which is probably what the Aborigines thought who shouted at him at the tea tree spring! He added that he would bring the sheep back from the lake once it was understood that it was on his land as it was too expensive for him to maintain an out-station up there. Next day the new arrivals left, 'grumbling that I meant to take a whole country to myself.'

Two days later, on 9 March 1840, two more Scots settled on the edge of his run. But he was confident he could force them off. 'Possession is the only sure claim here, and none can settle within less than three miles of an out-station, otherwise the Commissioner of Crown Lands will turn them off.' All one needed to claim a run otherwise was sufficient stock to put it all to use and a £10 license.

It was amazing how territorial and protective of his claims he quickly became. On 13 March he said he had no men to look after the sheep.

> Each man is out at a different point fending off intruders and we can hardly defend ourselves, but hope the worst of it is over as scabbed sheep are prohibited from travelling except in the month of February, and all the sheep at Port Phillip are scabbed. Donald McNicol has this moment come from the lake unwell and I must go 130 miles before I can get another [to keep guard].

Another of his tasks was to ensure that those there before him also moved out.

> On Sunday last, Donald Black and I fell in with a native chief's myoh myoh [native hut] – from the superior style in which it was built we judged it to be such. It was exactly the shape of a small potato, hurriedly and carelessly put up. The frame was made of the broken branches of trees covered with earth, and a small hole on the south end of it served for both door and window.
>
> We ordered it tumbled to the ground and a piece of paper folded up containing a small quantity of [gun]powder put into the end of a split stick and the other end stuck into the grounds

to show the natives that it was done by whites and we did not want them near us.

Ten days later a Mr White from Portland Bay 'came to my house – on his way to inform the Governor of an affray he had with the natives in which it is said forty-one of them had been killed.' He told Black his story.

About a fortnight ago, a large party of them came to one of the out-stations and took from the shepherd 900 breeding ewes ... Next day nine men set out after the blacks, five on horse and four on foot. When they had travelled about eight miles, they came across the native encampment. When the whites were seen approaching, they set up a tremendous yell and about thirty drew out in order of battle.

They were on the opposite side of a creek, and the first man that crossed the creek was speared through the leg and pinned to the ground. His friends followed him and soon dispatched the blackfellow. He fell after having nine balls lodged in his body – making signs to his friends to fight.

The fight lasted about an hour, spears against rifles. It took a great deal of courage for anyone to fight under such a disadvantage. But it was more evidently a massacre than a fight. For apart from the man speared through the leg – a traditional Aboriginal warning shot or punishment still used in some parts of Australia, which, when skilfully executed, does not cause lasting harm – no other whites were as much as scratched. The account continued.

The Protector of Aborigines was within six miles of that place at the time – and his report (collected among the natives themselves) is that forty-one have been killed, and Mr White says he is not aware of more than twenty-five. The bodies were all removed and put out of sight by the natives – a thing they never fail to do.

Sievwright, the Protector, collected a statement from one of White's men that 'between thirty and forty men, exclusive of women and children, were shot dead, only one escaping out of the whole tribe.'[7] The number of sheep stolen went down to 127 on investigation.

Black seems to have thought the whole affair justified. 'The whole of the sheep was recovered except forty-five they slaughtered.' The brothers White only arrived in January, two months before. 'They are only seventy miles distant from here but neither them nor I will ever be troubled with blacks again.' The whites 'may be obliged to go to Sydney to stand trial for murder, but it will be mere form. They must be acquitted.'

He was right. La Trobe accepted their statements without checking their accuracy, despite discrepancies. Sievwright's collected depositions were disallowed after the Crown Prosecutor argued that they were statements by the principals in the action and not by witnesses! Despite their admission that they had killed at least twenty Aborigines, they did not even have to stand trial. Next month the whites went out on another killing expedition.

Black seemed somewhat nervous about recording all this in his journal for his friends back home. He wrote:

> I had some doubts in my mind about making this entry, as it might occasion my friends some uneasiness on my account ... to overcome any foolish fears that might be felt by friends, I may here state that even one instance of natives attacking a home station has never yet been known in this colony, and several men lately on this establishment are now very ill with native pox, which shows how they acted with the blacks.
>
> I am told it is no uncommon thing for these rascals to sleep all night with a lubra and if she poxes him, or in any way offends him, perhaps shoot her before twelve next day.
>
> How can the father or husband feel upon such an occasion, or how can they avoid resentment at such usage? And I am certain it frequently happens.

He insisted that his diary was only for the eyes of his friends. He was concerned about repercussions if it were to be made public. There were still unwanted people on his claimed run. In a diary entry for 28 March he noted:

> Rode out to the lake to sheep washing, The natives paid them a visit this morning and made signs saying they wished to come to the hut, but the men showed them the guns and they made off. On my return here late in the evening heard that a flock of sheep was on the other side of the creek. I have scarcely time to eat my food, but flying from one part to another to keep off the enemy – civilized man. He is much more troublesome to me than the savage.

This latest incursion caused him to go up to town to complain to La Trobe. While there, he would take the opportunity of putting the finishing touches to his journal and sending it off to his friends in Scotland so they might know what faced them if they were to come out here.

Melbourne had grown in a fever of building while he was absent. 'I was away from this town for nearly two months. When I came back, I thought a magic wand had been waved over it. Where the forest stood when I left, there I found houses and streets on my return.'

His final diary entry, on 15 April 1840, described a great tournament among the Aborigines camped outside town.

About two o'clock, heard a tremendous yelling and saw every person running. At last I followed the crowd on being told three different tribes had assembled and were fighting a battle on the other side of the River Yarra Yarra half a mile distant, from which the yelling proceeded.

The battle appeared to me to resemble a game, or perhaps an ancient Scotch tournament, rather than a fight between hostile tribes. A few [Aborigines] sometimes stepped forward out of the crowd, and every inch of flesh on their bodies shook in the most extraordinary manner, by some power which I cannot exercise. Then the chiefs gave them orders, and a general movement and shifting took place throughout the whole, and spears, barbed with glass, flint or some hard metal stuck on with gum, were thrown at different times and in different directions, and when one was wounded on either side, the yelling commenced.

There was none speared through the body, and only three that I saw through the leg. The speared warrior was always supported by two of his companions, who held down their heads and looked steadily at the ground, while their arms were twisted around his body holding him upright, the point of his spears stuck in the ground and holding them in his right hand.

Their bodies and faces were all tattooed with strips of white and yellow clay, some trembled with cold, not one having a single shred on their bodies. Their hair was also plastered with clay and their appearance altogether hideous, but their gait and the beauty of their bodies noble and war-like.

After the fight ceased with the men, the lubras gathered together, and set up the most extraordinary cackling ever heard by mortal. They were also chiefly naked.

One only at a time appeared under the influence of the most fearful excitement. She would rush into the middle, shake her flesh and hair, her eyes sparkling, and her appearance indicating the wildest frenzy when, in one instant, she'd cool down and a more general but more moderate cackling commenced all round.

The fight is to be resumed in a few days more.

Black then sent his journal to Scotland. In return, he requested his friends to send him 'a few pairs of grey, home-made stockings, plaiden trowsairs and a cask of good Highland whiskey would be very desirable.' If they should send more, he added, it could easily be sold for a good profit.

*

Henry Meyrick next takes up the settlers' story. He arrived in Melbourne four days after Niel Black finished his journal. While Black went west, he went east of Melbourne to find himself a station – to the same parts as the Van Diemen's Land Aborigines were to attack. His meticulous correspondence back to his family in England painted a detailed picture of the life east of Melbourne on the Mornington Peninsula and in Gippsland between 1840 and 1846.

Meyrick came from a prosperous clerical family. His father was a minister of the Church of England with a parish in Wiltshire, as well as being a magistrate, a farmer and a sportsman who enjoyed archery and cricket. The family motto was *Heb Dhu, Heb Dhim, Dhu a Digon* (Have God, Have everything, God and Enough).[8]

Meyrick's letters were often beautifully inscribed, especially in the early days. They were written on two sheets of paper neatly folded, so as to dispense with the need of envelope, and sealed with wax. The ink is now faded to brown. To save paper, he sometimes wrote across the page from top to bottom as well as side to side. Later on he had to improvise with black swans' quills for pens and blacking for ink.

Meyrick came to Port Phillip with his cousin, Maurice, when they were both just seventeen. Both of them had a £1000 by way of capital. He wrote to his mother on arrival on 12 May 1840.

> Dear Mama, Here we are at last at the end of a six month voyage; we anchored here on Saturday and were by no means sorry to leave the good ship *China*.
>
> The steerage passengers here had not far to go to look for situations. The *China* was crammed with people from all sides looking for servants and in two days there was not one left except such as were going on to Sydney. Horses here are frightfully dear. A horse in England worth £15 or £20 is worth eighty here.

Meyrick was trying to get horses to take them down to Point Nepean where they had friends.

The population of Melbourne was now about 4,000. There were some 800 houses in the town. A million pounds of wool were sent back to England that year. Yet Melbourne, two years before, had been described as a 'nucleus of huts embowered in the forest foliage . . . like to a village seen in the interior of India.'[9] Over the previous three years land prices for blocks in the centre of Melbourne had risen from £35 to £5000 for half an acre. Land speculation was all the rage.

On 16 June the Meyrick cousins set out east to find themselves their runs. They went down across the creeks draining the Carrum Swamps to the Mornington Peninsula where Aborigines had long ago first met up with white settlers and had long since been subdued. William Buckley, who lived among Aborigines for thirty years before Melbourne was founded, stated that 'I always avoided going to Western Port to fall in with the sealers . . . these men ill-treated the blacks and were attacked and ill-treated in their turn.'[10]

Meyrick wrote:
Walked ten miles to Boniong where we shot kangaroos and minded the sheep for a week, then started on our first expedition into the bush to explore a run about thirty-six miles from Boniong called Colourt (near Sandy Point on Western Port Bay). We took no provisions with us, trusting to our guns. Our black guides were excellent hands at stalking kangaroo which we cut up and eat half raw.

We found an excellent run – a splendid river ranging through the middle of it, but unfortunately it is salt. It is, however, full of fish, and covered with ducks – we slept the night under a miah miah they knocked up.

He had only one request of his mother, which he made in a letter dated 16 June: 'Send three pairs of Wellington boots and a pocket compass.'

They purchased bullocks to pull their cart to bring in supplies. But it was very hard penetrating the dense Mornington bush. 'I do not quite know how we will get there, as the scrub is so thick in places we could hardly get there on foot.'

Sight unseen, they purchased a herd of cattle. They each bought eighty head for £600 each. They had to wait many months as the cattle had to be driven down from Sydney.

On 20 June he wrote:
My dear Mamma,
We are very lucky in the tribe of blacks around us. They are the only quiet set in the country. Their chiefs most of them

like Englishmen and call themselves gentlemans ... About the Goulburn, and on the Portland bayside, they are shot like dogs, whenever they are met with on account of their liking to mutton-pies.

Instead of Greek and Latin, I am learning Boneurong* and colonial.

He could not send a kangaroo as requested as they were 'altogether too cumbersome'. He was starting to put up huts and dig in potatoes and apologized for not being able to write for a while.

Life was difficult at his selected site. He could not find fresh water and his horse ran off and was not found for three months, so he beat an 'ignoble retreat from Western Port Bay.' But it was not long until he found somewhere new on the coast just beyond Mt Eliza. 'I heard of a place over the back of Mt Eliza, halfway between Melbourne and Boniong called by the Natives 'Narren-Guillen' (place of the hut?) where I am now beginning to get settled.' He got himself a whale boat to make it easier to get supplies from Melbourne than traversing the mud tracks and fords of the land route. He caught more fish, especially snapper, than he knew what to do with.

At first he lived in a tent. He wrote on 1 November 1840:
I am now sitting on a sugar-bag and making a table of a flour-bag, but as we have built a hut, we shall soon get into a more civilized way of life. At present there are four families of blacks with us. One a doctor of his tribe ... The only news was 'the blacks are playing up a bit on the Goulburn'.

In conclusion I will follow the example of Horace and give you a description of myself. I am 5'11" in height, burnt black with the sun, as strong as a bullock, with a great beard upon my face and I am so fat ...

The hut was finished, 'all but the chimney', but still 'the parrots can fly through the crevices.'

On 11 November he wrote:
'I have no news yet for you. The cattle are not yet come thou' we expect them any day. In one week more, I shall have

---

* This is alternatively spelt Bunnerong and was the name of the tribe which held the land from St Kilda up to the Yarra, along to Bald Hill near Gardiner Reservoir down to Andersons Inlet and back along the coast. Wilsons Promontory was common sacred ground with neighbouring tribe of Gurmai. Both Wurundgeree and Boneurong are dialects of Kulin language group.

attained the great age of 18. Instead of cake and wine, I must be contented with a glass of grog and that great bush luxury, commonly called "flopper in the pan", which is a sort of greasy pudding.

The cattle were not to arrive until January 1841.

He went into Melbourne for relaxation and supplies. On 7 January 1841 he commented:

There is a most marvellous change in Melbourne since I knew it first. The good old days of the bush are gone. No longer does the bushman enter Melbourne in an old shooting jacket, booted and spurred, nothing will do now but the splash dress-coat, in fact, the most complete puppyism has invaded the whole place.

Yet it was only six months since he arrived! He was not reluctant to take part in the high life. He concluded his letter with, 'Please send me three pairs of moleskin trousers and a dress-coat.'

On 20 March 1841 he was selling Narren Guillen for £100 as it was 'too mountainous'. He had been very ill with typhoid for over two months and had been put on a milk diet. They had been back to visit their first run at Colourt – and had found fresh water. So they were going to move back.

Once more this hardy squatter of nine months lamented the change in Melbourne town. 'The good old days are completely gone; no longer does the squatter ride up to town in a short jacket with one spur. The tracks of gig wheels are too often seen where formerly a bullock dray could not go.'

The bush had changed too. 'The bush is swarming with ladies now, a thing unheard of when I first got here.' The Mornington Peninsula was quiet, with no militant tribes. It was looked on as a safe and secure place for the gentry to settle, so out they came by bullock cart and horse, bringing with them pianos and silverware.

There is a very nice family half way down 'tween Narren Guillen and Melbourne. Major Fraser, Mrs and Miss Fraser and young Frasers . . . They have a beautiful piano and Miss Fraser sings very nicely; she is the belle of Melbourne and is engaged to be married.

On 10 September 1841 he wrote to Mama from Colourt using a feather, a 'black man's quill', about the ease of getting servants. They were now coming in daily by ship. The gentry used to crowd out to the steerage quarters on arriving ships to compete for servants. Many were arriving and the new hands had reduced the rate of wages from £50 per annum to £30, which made a considerable difference to the squatters.

The citizens of Melbourne seemed more concerned about the conditions of their streets churned up by horse, cart and bullock than about the Aborigines. They complained about wild cattle being driven down Queens Street. A tailor had to run for his life and narrowly escaped.

After heavy rains the streets of Melbourne were seas of mud. In Little Flinders Street, 'a horse, water cart and man were invisible for a short time having slipped into an immense cavity in the middle of the road filled with sludge.' They were rescued with great difficulty – the man with an improvised life raft, the horse by dragging itself out with help from nearby onlookers. As for the cart, half a dozen teams of bullocks were needed to pull it out. In front of the *Herald* office, three horsemen were spilt and drays sunk to their axles.[11]

The border wars seemed remote and of little concern or hindrance, although the *Port Phillip Herald* of 29 October 1841 reported constant attacks in the direction of the Grampians. In July the papers were filled with items such as the collection of money for Scots Church, and how a delicious wild turkey, six feet long, had been caught and eaten.

They were also concerned about the idleness of the prisoners at the gaolhouse. 'We are happy to tell the public that every preparation is being made to have a treadmill. The building has been commenced immediately outside the walls of the new gaol.'[12] In the same month there was a highway robbery on Sydney Road, twenty-five miles from town. 'A white man and a black man over seven feet tall have been apprehended.'

There was much controversy over the size of the New Melbourne Gaol, then under construction. It intimidated the inhabitants of the Melbourne settlement. They saw it as a spectacular eye-sore. It loomed over the settlement from out in the bush north of Lonsdale Street, spoiling a 'verdant plateau' of 'luxuriant gum and she-oaks'. It's very size was seen as a Sydney-imposed threat, large enough to imprison much of the population. (The building constructed at that time is, today, the southern wing of the Old Melbourne Gaol.) Lonsdale Street was Melbourne's border, with only four huts between Flemington and Fitzroy.[13]

Such was some of the gossip and the concerns of Melbourne Town, while out on Mornington Peninsula things were no longer so good.

There were the first signs of a crash, a failure of the fragile credit economy constructed by the first settlers. Intermittent heavy rains and droughts were taking their toll. Many settlers did not have the financial reserves to weather any form of crisis.

On 25 November Meyrick reported that Anderson's and Hind's stations had failed. Others were in trouble. He commented: 'Melbourne, in which the crisis is fast approaching, either a very sudden change must take place or the kangaroo will again drink at the Yarra.'

Also in November, the price for sheep fell from three pounds each when they arrived, to eighteen pence each. Yet the immigrants were still pouring in. 'There are 1500 emigrants landed and some still in the bay.' In the following twelve months, the white population of Port Phillip was to double to 20,000.

Aboriginal resistance to settlement rapidly increased as the flood of immigrants spread over their land. Henry Meyrick in this same letter recounted his first experiences of the frontier wars. He wrote to Reverend Meyrick (probably his father) of Hungerford, Wiltshire, from Colourt Station on Western Port Bay, 25 November 1841.

> The whole neighbourhood has been thrown into the utmost confusion, as the newspapers would say, by 3 VDL [Van Diemen's Land] blacks, who were brought over as servants by Robinson, the Chief Protector, and ran away, making common cause against all white men. They murdered four and robbed Allen's station which is ten miles from Colourt.
>
> They have just been taken and will doubtless be hanged. Had they come on to Colourt we would have robbed the hangman of his fee for we had guns loaded enough to have annihilated a whole tribe.*

The Aborigines brought across by Robinson to 'civilize' the Victorian Aborigines for the settlers had instead taken to the gun to fight the settlers alongside Victorian Aborigines.

---

* Meyrick's story is continued in Chapter 9.

Chapter Four
Melbourne Protected

When the Aborigines arrived from Flinders Island in January 1839, an epidemic of influenza was raging around Port Phillip. Most of the blacks had deserted Melbourne to try to escape infection as, unlike Europeans, they had no immunity to it. In any case, it was their normal custom to move camp if anyone died. Robinson himself was ill with influenza and could not leave the ship in Port Phillip for four days after he arrived. It was possible that he had introduced the epidemic to Flinders Island when he arrived back from Sydney to collect the Aborigines, several of whom died there from 'flu around that time.

It was not long before the Aborigines began returning to Melbourne. William Thomas recorded in his journal on 17 January 1839. 'Saw several blacks. The inhabitants of Melbourne say that they are returning to the settlement, having left it on account of the influenza that prevailed. The natives consider that the whites brought the disorder.'[1] They were soon back in large numbers. Robinson attributed this to their desire to have a 'conference' with him. Certainly they had received confusing stories about him. Some had told them that the Protector would right their wrongs and look after their needs. Others had recounted stories of Robinson's exploits in Tasmania, making the Aborigines wary of him. They feared that he might plan to remove them from their land to a remote settlement, or to poison them.

William Thomas recorded: '12 February. From this date to the end of the month, the blacks began by great numbers to visit the settlement. Waworong and Port Phillip tribes encamp on the south side of the Yarra between us and the falls (at the wharf).'[2] The Assistant Protectors set up their tents along this south side of the river while Robinson took over an old police hut. The Van Diemen's

Land natives were left to put up grass shelters for themselves nearby. This was a traditional Aboriginal camping area.

Robinson's assistants had been appointed by the British authorities directly; none had been to Australia before. Three were middle-aged Methodist school teachers. Their names were James Dredge, William Thomas and Edward Parker. The fourth, Charles Sievwright, was a former military officer who had to sell his commission to pay gambling debts. They had arrived in Melbourne shortly before Robinson, after a eighteen-day journey by ship from Sydney.

Robinson, with their help, organized in February a 'great feast' of beef, mutton and bread for the Aborigines with competitive games, food and fireworks. He also invited all the townsfolk and most came. The Aborigines had to be re-assured that the food had not been poisoned to get rid of them. Thomas reported that

> some evil-disposed person ... bid the blacks not eat anything for the feast was only a trap, they would eat and then be stupid and all would be taken prisoners ... no report could have operated so strongly upon the blacks, for in this infant state of the district, many, it was said, up the Ovens and Broken Rivers had been put aside this way.[3]

They were reassured and 'the afternoon was spent in blacks wrestling, climbing up poles, throwing spears at hats, etc.' Robinson's purpose in throwing the feast was to let the tribes know that he had come with good intentions. The tribes also took it to mean that the Protectorate would supply free rations and other goods, which the Aborigines saw as proper, given the talk of justice and compensation. However, rations were to be severely limited. The Colonial Secretary wrote to La Trobe on 21 October 1839.

> The Governor, Sir George Gipps, being of the opinion that large or general issues of food or clothing to the Aborigines are mischievous as tending to lessen the inducement which they would otherwise feel to work for wages, His Excellency requests that the articles may be supplied in small quantities.

Robinson reassured La Trobe by explaining his philosophy. 'They should be taught to feel their wants, should feel their necessities; a desire for civilized comforts and for the possession of property should be created ...'[4] Rations, he concluded, should only be given to the weak and sick.

By now there were some 500 Aborigines assembled on the Yarra camping grounds. Many tribes had come together. During the days

The house of William Thomas, Assistant Protector. Thomas is at the far right, *Mitchell Library, State Library of New South Wales*

A typical squatter's home on the Mornington Peninsula in the 1840s

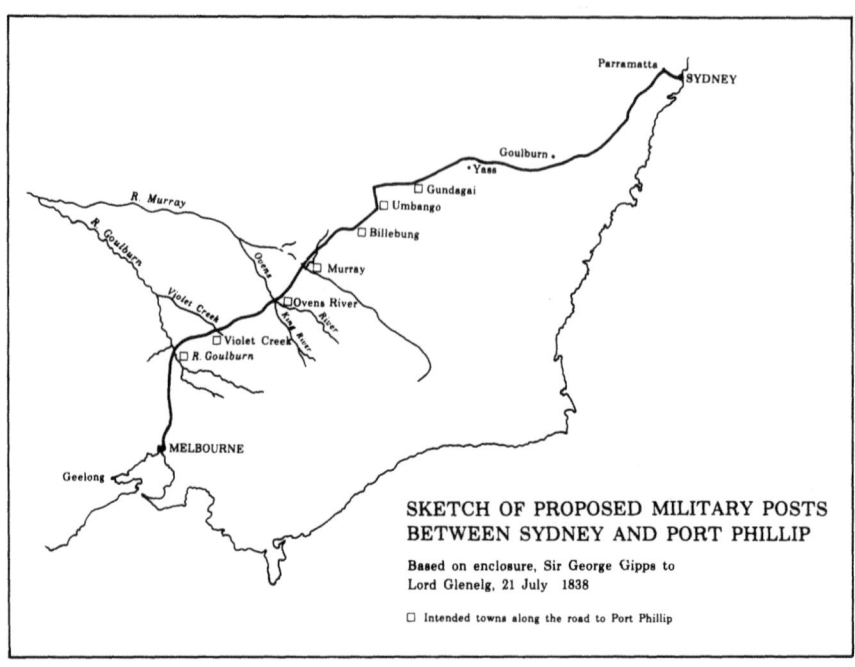

Historical Records of Victoria, Victorian Government Printing Office

William Thomas's drawing showing where a massacre of Aborigines took place near Mt Rouse, *La Trobe Library, State Library of Victoria*

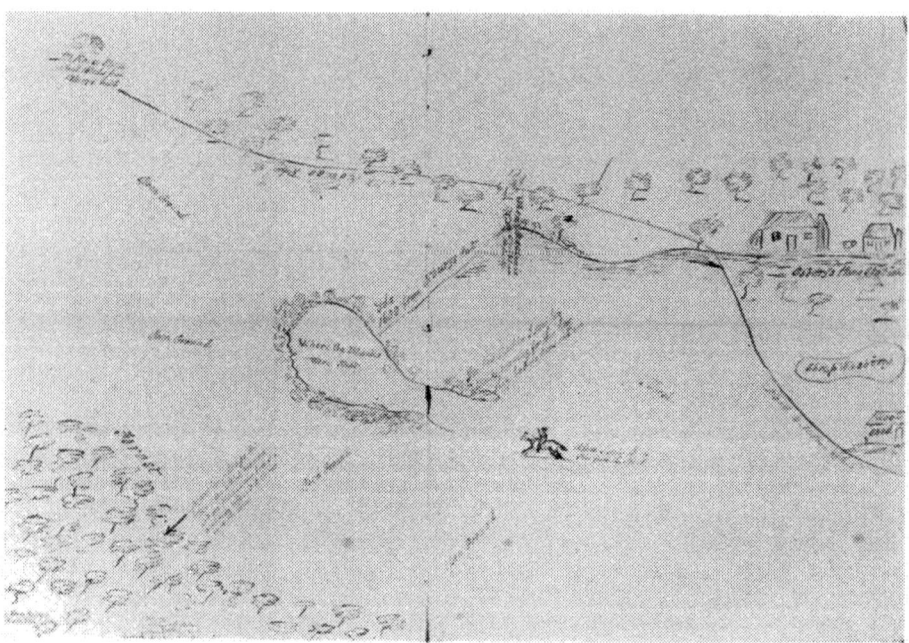

Windberry, shot in October 1840 during a mass arrest at the Yarra encampment, William Thomas's pencil sketch, *La Trobe Library, State Library of Victoria*

thank Heaven. The whole neighbourhood has been thrown into the utmost confusion as the newspapers would say, by three V.D.L. blacks who were brought over as servants by Robertson the chief protector, and ran away,

making common cause against all white men, they murdered four, and robbed Allen's station which is ten miles from Tillowst; they have just been taken, and will doubtless be hanged: had they come on to Tillowst we should have robbed the hangman of his fee, for we had guns loaded enough to have annihilated a whole tribe, tho' at one time Alfred was down here by himself for a week. Doct. Alfred is just come home, he went to town from Geelong, the wool is to be started the day after tomorrow; Alfred brought me a letter from Emma, and ...

The Revd. J. Meyrick
Ramsbury
Hungerford
Wiltshire
England

By Lear to Sydney

Henry Meyrick Letter to England, 25 November 1841, Henry Meyrick papers, *La Trobe Collection*, State Library of Victoria

there were mock battles. The Protectors spent their days parading around the Aboriginal camps trying to prevent any violence, real or make-believe. Many settlers were critical of the Protectors for this, saying they should not interfere with native customs. At nights there were major corroborees. The townsfolk would come out and watch the dancing and the daytime fights, often encouraging them by bringing out alcohol to offer around – even on Sundays, much to the horror of the Protectors.

On 26 March 1839 Robinson allocated areas to his Assistant Protectors: Sievwright to the Western District, Parker to the Northwest or Loddon, Dredge to the North-east or Goulburn and Thomas to the Melbourne and Western Port areas. They did not leave for up to six months after their appointments, losing time as they tried to get the resources they needed from a tight-fisted government.

On 1 April the Assistant Protectors were ordered out into the field. Sievwright reported that month what he had found west of Melbourne. He had visited sixteen stations; of these, only one was owned by a person sympathetic to the Aborigines. 'At two of the sixteen I found skulls of Aborigines placed over the doors of the huts as if to warn the lawful owners of the land of their peril to approach.'[5] At another station, two blacks had been shot dead for, it seemed, no more than disagreeing with a white.

Robinson soon asked Thomas to return to Melbourne to oversee the Aborigines in the large, town camps. He blamed Thomas for not taking the Aborigines with him when he left for Western Port.

The numbers of Aborigines camping outside town had not diminished after Robinson held his party for them. It became plain that they had business of their own to transact; they were not merely gathering to see what the Protectors were about. The major reason was to settle their own disputes. These were dealt with first by argument and perhaps tests of fighting skill but finally by one of their great dances traditionally used for the final settlement of disputes.

The Reverend Orton recorded in his journal on 19 April 1839:

> It appeared that some disagreement had induced several tribes to assemble on the bank to the amount of from four to five hundred to settle their disputes by fighting and corroborees according to their custom – for several nights. It appeared to be part of their design ... for the tribes to

corroboree or dance to each other as an extended mark of respect ... on other occasions the whole of the tribes assembles in one general corroboree.[6]

The famous Alpine dance of the Gaggip was a powerful peacemaker. Thomas was told that it consisted of seven different dances. In each except the last, a different weapon, and one only, is used. In the last dance, 'a bough, the emblem of peace' is used. When all the dances are finished, perhaps after many days, the symbols are put together in the centre of the encampment in silence, 'proclaiming good will to all around."[7] Thomas was told that 'When one tribe has Gaggip with another, from that time they are friends.' He was further told that the tribes were taught this dance and others by a community which lived in the Australian Alps. He quoted an Aborigine from Devils River.

There is a race of Blacks who live in stone houses made by themselves (not caves) and some of these Blacks never go out to seek their food like other Blacks but eat herbs and what Blacks give them, and these Blacks are very good – like our Sunday, and they teach ... dances and singing.[8]

Increasingly, Robinson centred his concerns on organizing his government department and less on the immediate care of Aborigines. He passed all the responsibilities he could to Thomas, reproving him when any complaints came about the Aborigines near Melbourne.

The Van Diemen's Land Aborigines found themselves not wanted. Since all Robinson's efforts to get rations for them had failed, several were loaned out to work for Robinson's sons or for other settlers. Two of the men went on droving trips to South Australia.

Late in April, Thomas recorded the following comments in his journal.

On the 26th accompanied Mr Robinson ... to see a party who had come overland from Sydney to Melbourne. They arrived on the 18th instant after fourteen weeks' journey ... Mr Hill described the disposition of the settlers towards the blacks, which he said in nine cases out of ten, was that of enmity. In more stations than one, three or four he could mention, they openly avowed their willingness to destroy them, and since the execution at Sydney they were more incensed than ever, and he had every reason to believe that many had been poisoned. In fact, at many of the stations, blacks would not partake of bread or milk or flour, fearing they should be poisoned.[9]

The Van Diemen's Land Aborigines must have felt at home! The blacks they had been introduced to along the Yarra were chronically ill with an influenza epidemic and dysentery. William Thomas, after holding a service for the Van Diemen's Landers on 5 May, went down to the Yarra camps.

A scene truly appalling presented itself; five were in the last stage of dysentery, [it was] a piercing cold night and . . . not a blanket to cover them.[10] [Next day a doctor visited and said that] In his whole experience of eighteen months . . . he never visited them in such a diseased and wretched state of want and disease, that five or six have already died and that five or six more are at the verge of death, and that unless something is done to relieve their wants, speedy extinction must soon take place.[11]

The large camps of Aborigines just outside the settlement were, by all accounts, a horrifying scene of illness, demoralization and desperation. Many had stayed on after the dancing because of illness. Settlers used to take pleasure in getting them drunk and in using the women as prostitutes. Many could not hunt because of ill-health and were forced to live by begging. The loss of tribal lands had shattered many. There were frequent inter-tribal fights as dispossessed tribes sought to find land the whites had not yet occupied. Assistant Protector Sievwright reported the state of Aborigines on the Yarra bank to Robinson on 5 May 1839.

In addition to a venereal disease, of which nine-tenths are the victims, and which appears under a more violent form than even the most extraordinary European cases, and from which neither age nor sex are exempted (as its ravages extend from the infant at the breasts to the decrepit and aged) they are now generally suffering from severe dysentery and influenza which appear to be rapidly extending among them.

The accumulation of so much disease . . . prevents the sufferers from supplying their own wants and those of their families by the usual means of the chase, and consequently leaves them dependent upon the capricious and uncertain support of the inhabitants of the township, who have been for some time past inclined to withhold their usual pittance in the hope of getting rid of the unusual number . . . Six had died in the previous four days.

Dr Cussen reported next day that the Aborigines were suffering from dysentery with typhus fever, syphillis and acute catarrh. 'To these horrors are to be added famine . . . and cold.'[12] At night, the temperature dropped below freezing.

When Robinson sent these reports to England, saying that the Aboriginal population had greatly declined since the European arrival, the Colonial Secretary noted, 'This surely could not have been the result of European settlement, but rather that of natural causes.'[13] The Governor, in response, ordered William Lonsdale to provide Robinson with relief supplies 'as may be absolutely required.'[14]

However, the Aborigines managed to keep their sanity. Their traditions demanded that they regularly visit different hunting grounds, so most of them departed Melbourne at the end of May.[15] But it was not long before some returned to live on the fringe of this alien, strange and prosperous town. The Aborigines showed a great deal more cultural curiosity than the whites. Many of them taught themselves English. Few settlers learnt an Aboriginal tongue. The constant movements of the Aborigines continued for years to frustrate Robinson's plans to make them settle down and become 'civilized'.

The local Superintendant, La Trobe, seemed to conceive of Robinson's role as being responsible for keeping the Aborigines out of Melbourne Town. La Trobe put constant pressure on Robinson to stop the Aborigines approaching town and even to remove the Aborigines from traditional camping grounds on the banks of the Yarra. Aborigines were actually forbidden to enter the infant town without permission.[16]

Robinson, in his turn, tried to shift the blame to William Thomas who was then trying to set up his Aboriginal Station, as ordered by Robinson, in the assigned area east of Melbourne. Thomas had chosen a site near Arthur's Seat on the Mornington Peninsula. Robinson told La Trobe that Thomas should have persuaded the Aborigines camped on the Yarra River to go with him.

Meanwhile, Thomas's supplies on board a cart had gone astray. He travelled south-east, past where Frankston now is, without water or food. He tried to get water by digging, but it was too salty. Eventually he arrived at the first station, Mr Hobson's, some forty-eight miles from Melbourne, met up with Aborigines and told them he was coming down to live among them. He went to 'visit Merrick's about sixty-six miles from the settlement [Melbourne]'.[17] This was near where Meyrick was to come to settle next year. Five days later still no supplies had arrived. He wrote in his journal on 21 August 1839:

> Visited a blacks' encampment where I remain this day without provisions. Very uneasy, not liking to live upon the

settlers. I made up my mind to leave the following day to go to Mr Jimmerson's, a fellow passenger, at Cape Schanck.

He nearly died in the midst of the wilderness that was the Mornington Peninsula. He was lost for days without water and was fortunate to survive. He had not travelled alone in the bush before. He recorded his adventure in his diary.

> 22 August. I imprudently proceed to find out Cape Schank without compass or road. Not in the least anticipating a want of water, I passed this day without water and, having no means of getting fire, at night lay me down in prayer.
>
> 23 August. This morning, after committing myself in prayer to God, commenced my wanderings . . . by night began to feel strange sensations in my head . . .
>
> 24 August. On my rising felt so ill and was awfully struck with God's preservation for I found I had been laying on a cluster of myrtles by a precipice of 40 ft at least. Was scarce able to walk, I never expected to see human beings again. I could not eat but chewed grass to allay my thirst. Night came again. I scarce lay down but I felt a spit of rain . . . In about an hour it rained hard. I caught rain in my handkerchief and, oh, what delicious fare!
>
> 25th August. My strength had gone and I could but walk slow. I thought if I could but get upon some rise and see the sea I should be right . . . [if I then] keep the sea on my right I should come to Arthur's Seat. After following rise after rise without success, I was forced to sit down . . .
>
> An immense eagle . . . came and hovered over me. Kept hovering . . . Heavens, methought, the bird will attack me . . . Fear aroused me. I got up, brandished my stick over my head and made for the next rise. He kept over me. This bird followed me, for I should say an hour at least, in which time I had made much ground through fear and excitement, and coming on a rise I saw the sea.[18]

When Thomas returned to the camp, the cart with his supplies had arrived. However, Robinson was quite unsympathetic to his misadventure. He told him he should have taken an Aborigine as a guide, and ordered him back once more to Melbourne to take charge of the Aborigines and to try to move them from the vicinity of Melbourne. Robinson complained that the Aborigines were constantly bothering him and hindering him in his work of administering a government department.

For several days now my office has been completely beset by them ... Repeated complaints of ill usage by white persons have also been made to me by these unfortunate creatures ... Your attention to keeping the natives from the township is requested.[19]

Thomas returned to town to find Robinson had 'harassed Mrs Thomas during my absence with threats of dismissing me for not obeying and answering his officials before I had or could receive them.'[20] Thomas protested most strongly.

Thomas was allowed the unusual concession of distributing rations free of charge to Aborigines at his Mornington Peninsula camp. This was solely to encourage Aborigines to go there from the Melbourne Yarra camps. The Van Diemen's Land Aborigines would sometimes stay on Thomas's station with the local Aborigines.

The white authorities were nervous about Aboriginal resistance spreading to the outskirts of Melbourne. Robinson gave strict instructions to Thomas to seize any guns he found in the possession of Aborigines. He protested against whites giving guns to Aborigines so they could hunt lyre-birds for their tails. Many merchants were making good profits from this trade but the Protectors and authorities saw it as short-sighted. Robinson wrote to the Assistant Protectors on 8 July.

It is very apparent that the Aboriginal natives are not in a situation to be entrusted with firearms. Their ideas of morality and notions of rectitude are of the most vague and uncertain description ... the frequent appearance of Aboriginal natives with firearms ... may endanger the lives not only of the black but of the white inhabitants also.[21]

However, the Protectors found it extremely difficult to disarm the Aborigines without any police to help them. Thomas reported that the guns would vanish into the bush on his appearance.

La Trobe's ban on Aborigines coming into the vicinity of Melbourne was equally hard to enforce. It was made without any regard for Melbourne being a newly founded settlement on Aboriginal land. The Aborigines carried on organizing their lives without taking into regard his prohibition. The banks of the Yarra River contained a number of very important ceremonial sites used by all the tribes. In 1840 the tribes decided they should meet again for a major ceremony at the traditional Yarra grounds. They had much to discuss, including the future of their people, how they could best protect their people and their remaining lands, the loss of hunting grounds and the frictions between the tribes.

On 17 August 1840, Robinson reported to La Trobe that the Goulburn tribes were on their way towards Melbourne, coming for a 'grand corroboree'. Next day he reported that, as instructed, he had met the Aborigines travelling into Melbourne, 'and remonstrated with them on the impropriety of their coming without permission.'[22] Shortly after he wrote again to say, 'immediately on receipt of your instructions I again visited them' and told them 'they were not permitted to visit Melbourne nor to remain in its immediate neighbourhood.'

La Trobe would have been particularly concerned about the Goulburn Aborigines coming to town. In April he had received a letter from a settler at Yea, Peter Snodgrass, telling him that attacks on the settlers along the Goulburn River were being carefully planned and co-ordinated. Snodgrass said the leader was Winnaberrie, a Wurundjeri man with tribal links to the Aborigines in Melbourne. 'He appears to have supreme command over the natives of this district and has been present aiding and assisting in all the attacks they have made on my men and my stock.'[23]

The Aborigines did not head directly for the camps near town, but headed up river to where Assistant Protector Thomas had set up camp at the junction of the Merri Creek and the Yarra near another Aboriginal meeting ground.

He had selected this site because it had been reserved from subdivision by the town authorities so it could eventually be the site of a prison or a mental hospital – for it was surrounded by the rivers on three sides. (This site is now used by the Fairfield Infectious Diseases Hospital and the Fairlea Women's Prison.)

On 28 August Robinson wrote La Trobe another flowing, copious letter telling how he had gone to the lagoons at Bolin (now Bulleen Ponds), thirteen miles from Melbourne, where some 200 Aborigines were camped, and how he had 'pointed out the impropriety of choosing a spot so close to Melbourne.' La Trobe commented that Robinson seemed to spend his time writing letters and not acting, but Robinson at least refused to use force to move them on.

Instead he travelled up the Yarra some fifty or sixty miles from Melbourne to see if he could find a camping ground safe for the moment from white incursions. He found a place near Healesville, but could not persuade the tribes to leave for there, even though the arrival of settlers meant 'there is but little game within twenty miles of Melbourne.'

Thomas was extremely concerned at the way all the land near the town was being subdivided without any regard for Aboriginal usage. He was particularly concerned about the Bolin lagoons from where Robinson had failed to move the people. He wrote to Robinson. 'When Bolin, and the few lagoons adjacent, becomes private property it will be one of the most serious losses hitherto sustained by the blacks.'[24] He expressed his dismay to the Governor directly in June 1841, when he heard these lagoons near Heidelberg were being sold to a land speculator, Frederick Unwin. He pointed out that the lagoons supplied a major part of the food of the local Aborigines who built permanent eel traps giving them a regular, easy harvest.[25]

On 5 September, Robinson tried to remove the blacks from the north bank of the Yarra (at what is now the Northcote side of Yarra Bend Park). 'I am sorry to say there is a growing spirit of dissatisfaction among them.' On 16 September he reported that he 'broke up the camp' when he found Aborigines still on the northern side of the river.

According to Thomas, in their meetings with other tribes, the Yarra Aborigines were then considering open warfare against the invading whites. He said that Billibellary, a Wurundjeri elder, advised against this, in the vicinity of Melbourne at least, because of the numbers of armed townsmen and troopers now present.[26]

Down at Geelong the resistance of the tribes was making life very difficult for the settlers. At a public meeting in North Geelong on St Valentine's Day 1840, a resolution calling for government assistance was carried unanimously:

> The settlers in this district, having severely suffered by the aggressions of the Aboriginal population which have been allowed to pass with impunity, deem it highly expedient to make an earnest appeal for the adoption of efficient measures to prevent their recurrence.

Not just military help was wanted. A further resolution, passed by a large majority of the meeting, stated that the only effective way of preventing the recurrence of such events is to feed and clothe the Aborigines sufficiently.

A mounted, para-military border police, using convicts with a military background, men who had deserted during the American War of Independence, was set up to protect the settlers and, on 29 August 1840, Governor Gipps proclaimed, 'Whereas the Aboriginal natives have obtained possession of firearms and it is considered dangerous to public security ... it is not lawful for any Aborigine or half-caste to have firearms or ammunition unless with the written permission of a Justice of the Peace.' Furthermore, it was legal for any 'free person' to seize firearms from Aborigines.

Meanwhile, the Assistant Protectors were growing increasingly frustrated. They had been made Justices of the Peace but received instructions that they could only take legal proceedings in cases directly involving Aborigines, and then only with the consent of the authorities. They soon discovered that evidence from Aborigines had no force at law, so that whenever whites killed Aborigines, only if there were other whites present that were willing to give evidence could any prosecution succeed.

They were also to find that many accusations of atrocities by Aborigines reported in the Port Phillip newspapers had no basis in fact. It was common for such stories to be invented to cover up neglect by shepherds or atrocities against Aborigines.

Sievwright was the first to discover this. He was sent to 'protect' the Aborigines around Geelong and further west. He investigated a report of sheep killing near Mount Piper. He reported on 16 March 1839, 'I am convinced the whole affair originated in the ... pusillanimous conduct of the shepherd, who, upon the appearance of the blacks, deserted his flock.'[27]

Assistant Protector Parker, who had been sent into the Mount Macedon district, investigated the killing of six Aborigines by troopers in May. It seems that two shepherds were attacked by Aborigines; one was killed, the other vanished. The settlers then called in the troopers who eventually found a party of Aborigines some sixty miles away, attacked them and killed at least six.[28] (One report said that forty –all the tribe save a woman and child – were killed.)[29] There was no evidence to indicate that they were the same Aborigines who attacked the shepherds. No prosecutions followed.

Assistant Protector Dredge, sent to the Goulburn River district, reported that he heard from settlers that things were worse the previous winter. 'Then the Aborigines took away one of their flocks, amounting to some 800 or 900 sheep, and ... thirteen of the blacks were shot before the sheep were recovered.'[30]

Dredge recorded in his diary that at Hamilton's Station, Mr Mundy shot men women and children of the Thongworong tribe in 'wholesale murder, another instance of the savage barbarity of *"white gentlemen"* toward the unprotected.'[31] Another Assistant Protector, Parker, said of the Mt Macedon district, that Aborigines were 'denied the rights of humanity – treated as wild dogs.'[32]

Sievwright charged two shepherds with shooting two Aborigines on Bowerman's station near the Julian Range 160 miles north-west of Melbourne. However, the Attorney-General refused to charge them with murder because they pleaded self-defence, the Aboriginal bodies had been burnt by the shepherds, and because there was no white person to give evidence against them.[33]

In November he reported that Aborigines had told him of a massacre of twenty to thirty Aborigines beyond Lake Corangamite. He said he would go immediately to investigate, but needed transport for his tent and supplies as it was some ninety miles away. The Reverend Benjamin Hurst said he too had heard of the murders from Aborigines.[34]

La Trobe gave Sievwright permission to hire a horse, but got very irate when he heard that Sievwright had not left earlier to investigate. Sievwright replied that he 'had applied to every settler within ten miles of my tent without success';[35] none would hire him a horse. Eventually he bought a horse at his own expense and went to investigate. It had been raining hard and the rivers were in flood.

> I had not proceeded twenty miles on this journey when it required three days to pass the first ford. Myself and servant had to carry everything across upon our shoulders, and even the beast, by great personal exertion, had to be drawn by us inch by inch through the swampy ground.[36]

By the time he got to the reported site of the massacre he could find no evidence. It was far too late. The nature of the country, the restrictions on prosecutions, the non-acceptance of Aboriginal evidence and the refusal of adequate means of transport, made it practically impossible for the Protectors to do their job.

Chapter Five
Melbourne Aborigines Take Up the Gun

When, in July 1839, Robinson wrote to the Assistant Protectors asking them to disarm the Aborigines, he mentioned an alarming rumour that had reached him indicating that Europeans had armed Aborigines to send them against tribes they wished to destroy.[1] He wrote that 'numerous reports of this kind had already reached me' from the most respectable of sources.

Setting Aborigine against Aborigine was one of the most effective tactics available for the settlers, for it neutralized the great Aboriginal advantage of their knowledge of the bush. It was employed by the government in their use of native police and trackers, capitalizing often on pre-existing hostilities. They would rarely try to use Aborigines in their own tribal areas against their own people.

At that time Aborigines were as conscious of national differences between one tribal group, or confederacy of tribes, as Europeans are of the differences between French and English, Spanish and German. The settlers were able to capitalize on pre-existing hostilities or to utilize Aboriginal mercenaries from distant parts.

Later that month, July 1839, Sievwright was searching for a party of seven Yarra Aborigines armed with guns. Thomas had told him they had left the Yarra for his area around Geelong. It was thought they were responsible for the earlier murder of an Aboriginal youth at Colac. He met up with them and reported that the group was now thirteen strong and that all the local tribes, on hearing of their coming, fled south to Indented Head.

On 24 July, Assistant Protector Parker wrote to Robinson to tell him that these Aborigines 'had been to Geelong and its neighbourhood where they had been employed by some persons . . . to shoot a number of the Manimet tribe in the vicinity of Lake Colac.'[2]

A group of some seventeen armed Aborigines had left the Yarra camp while Thomas was lost down on Mornington Peninsula. These may have included some of those who were earlier around Geelong. Robinson had been upset because Thomas was not around to deal with them. Thomas arrived back just as a group returned.

> They all crossed the punt, spears up and as silent as statues, fourteen in all. After crossing the Yarra they broke into two bands, six going to the Bonurongs and eight to the Yarra Tribe, spears up and as regular as soldiers would march.[3]

Thomas went up to them to try to find out what they had been doing.

> I went up to them and spoke but they made no answer. I pretended to feel for them and made them a fire. I watched narrowly, expected to see some portions of a fellow creature, but they, perceiving my anxiety, said, 'You go home. Black fellows want to talk.'

Next day Thomas saw many of them had guns but 'they were too deep to let me know from whom they received them. One black was learning his lubra to fire a gun.'[4]

From Thomas's inquiries he found that two Murrumbidgee Aboriginal youths who had taken jobs with white people had been murdered. It seemed that this degree of collaboration with the occupying whites was not acceptable. Thomas tricked Aborigines into telling him who was responsible. He pretended to an Aboriginal elder that he knew all about it and was sympathetic, thus getting him talking.[5] But later they found out Thomas had reported them to Robinson.

> One intelligent black told me almost verbatim what I had written to the Chief Protector. This is too bad; a Protector is ordered to enquire among savages and then exposed to the consequences.[6]

> The consequences were that the inquiry into these murders nearly cost me my life. The night following . . . one of my own blacks attempted to strangle me. On the following morning another was about striking me on the head with his tomahawk which I was successful in grasping 'ere the blow was struck.[7]

The first attempt was thwarted by someone riding up, the second by an Aboriginal elder giving him protection. Thomas was again refused any police assistance by Lonsdale, the Police Magistrate.

On 7 October, 'seven blacks (Yarra tribe) return from seeking bullen-bullen [lyre-birds]. Four had guns. They had no less than seventeen pheasant tails and many white people were about until dark trying to get the tails from them.' These tails were greatly prized by settlers who made much money from them. Next day Thomas found that

> sixteen more had come in with bullen-bullen. Going around I counted the guns in their possession which was twenty-six. As the order from His Excellency was to seize all guns in their possession, I sent to the Chief Constable information of the same. The Chief Constable sends word that he must not act without Police Magistrate's orders (query: what use is my J.P.?). I find five more stand of arms and write to the Police Magistrate.[8]

> I told the blacks that in consequence of blacks killing white men at Mount Macedon and other places, that Governor send all white gentlemen to prison who give black fellows guns, and take all blacks' guns, and that they had better give me their guns than have them taken by the Police, and I would send them to Police Office and they get money for them. 'No, no, no,' one and another cried, 'by and by big one hungry me.'[9]

The Aborigines prized their guns for hunting and self-defence. They would also have seen the manifest injustice of not also removing guns from the whites for killing blacks.

Thomas had a policy himself of never carrying a weapon. He said he hesitated in taking guns from Aborigines, for they had become 'a tool for his sustenance'. In any case, he did not think it prudent for him to try to remove them by himself.[10]

He camped in the middle of the Aboriginal Yarra encampment for about six weeks at this time. Tensions were running very high. Alcohol was being provided by a Melbourne trader and there were fierce fights between the Aborigines. On one occasion spears came flying right through his tent which he had refused to move. He then wrote to Lonsdale:

> I have written so much respecting constabulary aid without effect that I know not what language to urge to press its necessity. I beg to state once more that for the last week my life has been in daily jeopardy. I expect some lives will be sacrificed before the night is over. If you are disposed to save the lives of Her Majesty's subjects, I entreat you to let a few constables come and that immediately.[11]

Lonsdale once more did not lift a finger to help.

Thomas was not heard when he begged for the removal of two 'ferocious' blacks, members of the group who went to Geelong, suspected of murdering the two Murrumbidgee Aborigines. (They had committed the lesser crime of killing blacks.)

The town authorities would do nothing to remove the guns, either because it was seen as too dangerous an endeavour, or because the trade in lyre-bird tails and possum furs was too profitable to be abandoned. Several traders were making a fortune from this trade. Moreover, the Aborigines had not threatened any white people in Melbourne with their guns.

On 15 October 1839, Thomas asked if he could bring charges against a white man for murdering two Aborigines on Aboriginal evidence. He was told he could not. On another occasion, he was particularly angry and frustrated when he failed to get action despite having willing white witnesses.

> Walking up Little Collins Street, I observed a large dog rush from a butcher's shop upon two female blacks who were passing at the time and the butcher in place of calling off the dog appeared to encourage him. Indeed the females (one of them the wife of Jika Jika) declared to me that the man set it on them, of which I have no doubt.[12]

This time there were white witnesses, two highly respectable gentlemen, Mr Donald Gordon McArthur and Mr Henty. Had it not been for the 'humane exertions of these gentlemen the poor women must have sustained great injury. The two gentlemen willingly offered to appear and give evidence against the brutal conduct of the man.' They went together to see Lonsdale. But 'The Police Magistrate refused to grant a summons, stating that he would have nothing to do with aboriginal affairs.' So Thomas wrote out a legal summons and served it himself. Next day, the witnesses turned up – but not the accused – and Thomas could do nothing about it. Only when settlers were in danger did the authorities act.

La Trobe put all the responsibility for removing guns from the Aborigines on the unarmed Protectors, despite their pleas for help. On 28 October he demanded of Robinson that

> not a day be lost by you in depriving all ... of their firearms. I am quite persuaded that a firm and prudent exertion of your authority, personally exercised, would be sufficient, without any assistance from constables or other attendants whose very presence would imply the meditated use of force.[13]

He must have known this to be totally impractical.

He also requested the removal of the Aborigines camped near Melbourne for 'the considerable body of emigrants just arrived, must probably encamp on the same bank.' Governor Gipps commented that 'the stoppage of rations and allowance (to the whole [Protectorate] Department if necessary) will, I doubt not, compel the natives to remove.'[14]

Robinson replied:

> The expelling [of] the natives from the environs of the township, and the depriving them of the use of firearms, involves ... a question affecting the future peace and well-being of the white inhabitants of this rising province, and one in which the lives of many may hereafter be placed in imminent danger.[15]

Robinson saw these actions as a possible cause of conflict, if not handled with care and without violence. He claimed that his Protectorate's very existence 'has done good, for at no period within my recollection has the district and country of Port Phillip been in so tranquil a state and so free from native aggression.'[16]

But the fight had scarcely begun. As Aborigines were forced off more and more land they were forced to defend themselves and their land as best they could. Unrest grew rapidly in the Yarra Aboriginal camps. Tension rose. There was much drinking. La Trobe threatened to use 'decided measures' to force the 300 Aborigines camped outside Melbourne to leave. 'The continual location of such a numerous body of natives in the immediate vicinity of the town cannot be endured much longer.'[17]

Thomas formally recommended, as did Robinson, that a reserve be created so the Aborigines had some place of their own as a refuge and training centre. He noted that the local Aboriginal tribal lands would probably be entirely occupied by settlers within months.

> In August last there were but four settlers between Melbourne and Point Nepean. There are now [February 1840] nine, and I doubt not but from Melbourne to Western Port and along the banks of the Yarra have increased in the same proportion. Hence the necessity of an asylum and refuge as a covert from the inevitable crisis.[18]

On 3 January 1840, Thomas reported that in the Yarra camps 'a council took place of thirty-five, the greatest number I have known in council, of the principal men in each tribe, which lasted for near two hours. I soon learnt that their object was to remove altogether.'[19]

Most did leave next day. Thomas travelled with one large group towards WesternPort. About fifty were to hunt around Mt Martha and the Peninsula, and sixty more further around Westernport. He reported they kept away from all stations except one, 'the furthest in the district (Anderson's and Massie's excepted, in which direction the blacks never ever go).'[20] Thomas was mistaken or misled. It was precisely in that direction that a large group of armed Aborigines had gone.

As Thomas was struggling through swamps and boggy rivers with his bullocks and cart, trying to keep up with the Aborigines who had gone south-east, Anderson's station came under fire from Aborigines travelling up the banks of the Yarra. His station was near the present site of Warrandyte.

Immediately the authorities sent troopers to investigate. When they got to Anderson's they discovered about eighty Aborigines had gone on to Ryrie's station up at Yarra Glen and that seven of them were reported to be carrying guns. The troopers went on to Ryrie's.

Many of the Aborigines were out hunting when the troopers arrived, so the troopers hid their uniforms and laid an ambush with the aim of capturing the purported leader of the Aborigines. He was known to whites as Jackie Jackie. The ambush succeeded. Gisborne, the commander of the mounted police, reported:

> After a struggle of about ten minutes, three of them had succeeded in handcuffing and binding Jackie Jackie. He is a very tall, powerful man and made a desperate resistance. I hastily ordered him to be conveyed into a hut and watched, for by this time the blacks were returning in numbers from the camp with spears and muskets, and it was necessary for me to prepare a defence.[21]

It was a short-lived victory for the troopers. They charged at Aborigines who shot at them from a distance, but were lured into a swamp with Aborigines firing at them from impenetrable scrub on the far side. They returned to the hut to find that Jackie Jackie had escaped while they were away.

On 2 May, Bolden, the owner of another station on the Yarra, reported to La Trobe that on his station there were 'from two to three hundred blacks ... My men told me that last night the blacks threatened to burn the huts and drive the men away and at this time the blacks had from twenty to thirty guns and muskets.' When the troopers got there, they found the Aborigines had moved on.[22]

On 27 May Aborigines of the Goulburn River region raided Mackay's head-station killing a shepherd who had ill-treated their women, burning out-buildings and destroying stores and livestock. Later Lord Stanley in England was to determine that the 'fault in this case lies with the colonists rather than the natives.'[23]

But Governor Gipps sent in Major Lettsom and a detachment of troopers, giving Lettsom permission to take hostages if those responsible could not be caught.[24] He missed them but, finding they had gone to attend important ceremonies near Melbourne, he came down after them.

Because of these raids, legislation was swiftly passed to officially ban Aborigines from carrying guns. The proclamation did say that permits could be issued to Aborigines, but La Trobe wrote to Robinson to say that 'no permission under any pretext should be granted by the Magistrates of this district.'[25]

When Lettsom arrived in Melbourne he found over 400 Aborigines assembled for the ceremonies. He demanded that Thomas hand over a number of the more troublesome Aborigines. Thomas refused, as there was no warrant for their arrest and because the taking of hostages would set a dangerous precedent putting at risk all Aborigines.

Lettsom was angered at this. La Trobe, too, felt it was time to teach the Melbourne Aborigines a lesson. He saw no reason to respect the major religious ceremonies in progress in their camp. So, while Thomas was away investigating a robbery at WesternPort, La Trobe authorized the military to raid their camp in strength.

At dawn on Sunday, 11 October, Lettsom, accompanied by fifty-eight soldiers and police, pounced on the Aboriginal camp, arresting all there. One Aborigine was seen trying to escape. He was shot dead.

The *Port Phillip Patriot*, in a very short report, said that the man killed was Windberry whom Thomas described as a 'most splendid character'. Lettsom then destroyed all the Aboriginal hunting spears, their 'instruments of war'. He and his men *marched over two hundred of them* into Melbourne, '*pricking them with their bayonets and beating them with the butt end of their muskets.*'[26]

When he got to town, Lettsom had them all locked up in a warehouse. The Aborigines were angry and scared, expecting to be deported by ship to Sydney. During the night one of them was shot dead and another wounded while allegedly trying to escape. Thomas reported it was 'little more than murder. Nerruknerbook was shot while inside the store after being illegally detained under circumstances that encouraged escape.'[27]

Assistant Protector Parker managed to free all but thirty since no charges had been laid and the arrests were quite illegal. Twenty of the remaining thirty Goulburn blacks were freed a month later; no charge was laid against them either.

The remaining ten went before a magistrate. At the last moment Thomas was refused the right to interpret for them so they had no chance of any defence. La Trobe admitted that 'They were neither called on to plead, nor were they furnished with the means of formal defence.'[28]

Nine of them were found guilty of theft and sentenced to ten years' deportation. The evidence against them was offered by two convicts, one of whom had the vilest of reputations for abusing Aboriginal women. Aboriginal evidence was not admitted, nor even possible, without an interpreter.

However, the nine of them astonishingly managed to escape while on the way down the Yarra to the waiting ship. They got away despite their leg irons, which were later filed off by Yarra blacks.

With scant regard for legality, Gipps approved of Lettsom's actions and hoped it would prove a deterrent. 'I am in hopes that good results may be expected to follow.'[29]

But not everyone saw things this way. A letter appeared in the *Port Phillip Patriot* on 29 October 1840.

> Might I, after making my best bow to your highness of the PATRIOT enquire, as to whether, respecting the Aboriginal question, the officers of the law were justified in detaining the blacks who, by their non-selection from the general herd at the time the Goulburn desperadoes were picked out, were of truth declared guiltless, and who were only kept in restraint till it suited the convenience of the authorities to send them to the other side of the river and there release them?
>
> If they were not, then of truth the shooting of the old man in the government store must be designated something more than "justifiable homicide". When I say this I bear in mind that they had been inspected and judged by a magistrate and that the whole of the Yarra Yarra blacks were set at large.

These events had a major impact on the Aborigines. The camps outside town became still more militant. Some of the Aborigines urged their compatriots 'to go to the mountains and live, no more eat flour; like before the white man came.' (Translation made for W Thomas.) Others urged increased warfare.[30]

While all these events were happening, the Van Diemen's Land Aborigines had been widely dispersed. Robinson lost interest in them shortly after he had trouble securing funds to pay for their expenses, and when he found he could not easily control their movements, in particular, when he could not keep Truganini from spending nights with 'uncivilized' Aborigines.

Initially, right after the Van Diemen's Land Aborigines' arrival, he would take them with him to the Yarra camps and on picnics up the Yarra. But he soon sought other work for them so they would not be a charge on his own budget. Bob Timmy and Walter Arthur he sent off with Alfred Langhorne to assist him trek across to South Australia. Woorrady and the older men assisted on the properties belonging to Robinson's sons.

The women he found particularly hard to control, particularly Truganini. In August 1839 he objected to her and Charlotte spending the night in the Yarra Aboriginal camp. Then, in April 1840, when he left for a two-month journey inland, the Van Diemen's Land Aborigines dared to leave also. They were recaptured, but before Robinson returned, Truganini ran away with Charlotte for a second time.

Shortly after this Robinson told La Trobe he wanted the Aborigines returned to Flinders Island. In August he told La Trobe that they 'were no use to me and I wished to get rid of them.'[31] On 25 August he formally asked to be quit of them and La Trobe soon relieved him of all responsibility for them.

At the end of August Truganini was recaptured. At one stage she had been living with shepherds down on Point Nepean. She ran off again in November, this time with Matilda, and again she was recaptured.

It seems the Tasmanian Aborigines had plenty of opportunity to mix with the local Aborigines and to see what was happening. About this time some of them laid plans to wreak their own vengeance on the whites. A warning was passed on. In May 1840 William Thomas wrote:

> It was reported to me that a Van Diemen's Land Black from Flinders Island [probably Isaac] has been traversing over this district. He met with a good reception from the settlers having, as he stated, come to tell them that the five [illegible] Blackfellows were coming down – and bade them get plenty of guns ready.[32]

This warning was to prove quite accurate. By October, all the station owners and hands in the Mornington and Westernport districts were preparing their guns or escaping back to town.

It is not clear who gave the warning. One note, undated, from Thomas seems to suggest it might have been Isaac. 'I am informed by the Blacks . . . that the two Van Diemen's Land women are gone to Western Port after Isaac.'[33]

Others quickly followed. Jack of Cape Grim, who was Fanny's husband, left Melbourne, supposedly for Thomas's settlement, but vanished into the bush. Robert joined up with Truganini, with whom he was reportedly sleeping.

Certainly by August or September 1841 Truganini, Matilda, Fanny, Bob and Jack were all together in the bush, beginning their campaign to drive as many settlers as possible from the eastern tribal lands. The first newspaper reports said that they fought together with Victorian Aborigines.

Thomas's eldest son, also called William, remembered them well. He wrote of their motives in his journal.

> At length they tired of the monotony not being allowed to go about at their will. There was a man among them, a man superior in every respect to the others. He had been a leading man, a chief in his own country, and he was the leader of the malcontents here – his name was Napoleon [a name Robinson gave to Jack of Cape Grim]. He talked about what they had suffered at the hands of the white man, how many of their tribe had been slain, how they had been hunted down in Tasmania – now was the time for revenge, they were not cooped up in an Island, they had unlimited bush to roam over at their will – a woman Lalla Rooke [Truganini] aided him and abetted him.[34]

Chapter Six
The Tasmanians Fight

Lieutenant Samuel Rawson of the 28th Regiment was sent out in October 1841 to the remote and wild areas of Westernport to help protect the settlers. He built himself a base-hut on the northern shore of Western Port Bay near the mouth of a river, known to Aborigines as Kannang, today as Yallock Creek. Shortly after his arrival Mr Powlett, Commissioner of Crown Lands, came to visit with two policemen. Mr Powlett's job was to supervise the sale of former tribal lands to the settlers.

That same evening, at about five o'clock on 10 October 1841, Rawson and Powlett heard of events that would totally dominate every minute of their lives for weeks to come.

A boat came into shore nearby carrying two miners and their wives, and four whalers. They had come from Victoria's first mine, a small, cliff-face, coal operation near Cape Patterson which had only been open a few weeks. It was shipping coal to Melbourne from 'two seams of the finest quality'. The miners and the whalers had come seeking help because two whalers had been killed by a group of Van Diemen's Land Aborigines.

They had already appealed to La Trobe for help. A nearby station owner, a Mr Massie, had written for them to La Trobe relating how the group of Aborigines had raided the hut of the overseer of the coal mine while the men were away getting supplies. The Aborigines had ordered the women staying at the hut well out into the bush and 'then rifled the hut of its contents and set it on fire, taking with them two guns and ammunition.'[1]

Just after the Aborigines left, they were surprised by the overseer returning with his son-in-law, Walter Inman. Gunshots were exchanged, slightly wounding the son-in-law in the leg. The whites fled to Massie's station to get help.

Just a short while earlier, a party of seven whalers, walking from their base at Lady's Bay along the shore, had come across the deserted coal mining settlement. They searched for the miners and, seeing some people in the bush about 200 yards off, two of the whalers set off towards them.

Five minutes later two shots rang out. The main group of whalers saw several people running towards the beach. Thinking that these must be the miners out hunting, they decided to have a sleep in a hut until the miners returned. It was only when they woke up that they realized something may be amiss.[2]

Samuel Evans, one of the whalers, asked 'Where's Yankee and Cook?' No one had seen their two companions. They had not returned from going off to find the miners. So the others, in their turn, set out to search for them and for the miners.

They hadn't been searching for long when up came the rescue party raised by the mine overseer, Mr Watson, with guns at the ready. One of Watson's men fired a warning shot over their heads and the whalers immediately thrust their hands up in the air. As soon as they had identified themselves, the whalers asked if they had fired the two shots heard earlier. They said they had not. One of the new arrivals, Patrick, said he would go and look for the missing whalers while the others had a cup of tea.

In less than ten minutes he was back; he had found their bodies on the beach. William Cook had been killed instantly by a shot through the ear; Yankee had been shot in the side of his body, then killed with blows to the head. According to Massie, the Aborigines responsible were still around.

> The blacks were at this time on an adjacent hill making gestures. The men went in pursuit of them and kept them in view for several hours, but were unsuccessful in catching any of them. They are still in the vicinity.[3]

Massie's letter identified the Aborigines responsible as five who had stayed on his station for two weeks, leaving it only a few days before.

> The party consists of two men and three women. The men are named Bob, alias Jamie, and Jack, the latter a stout man and I believe a native of Cape Grim, Van Diemen's Land. The women are named Truganini, Matilda and Fanny. They evidently plundered some other hut before arriving at my station as they brought a large quantity of tea and sugar with them.[4]

The Tasmanian Aborigines were later to say that they had thought the men they killed were Mr Watson and his son-in-law out hunting them. A short time before they had exchanged fire with the Watsons. They then laid an ambush for them and the two whalers walked into it. Jack shot Cook and Bob shot Yankee. There were conflicting stories about who had beaten Yankee over the head. One report, published in a Port Phillip paper, said it was Bob's mate, Truganini, using a club made from tree roots. A policeman told the paper that Truganini had confessed to it.[5] Powlett and Johnson were to give evidence that Truganini said that it was Bob and not her.[6] Bob was to say that it was Jack *and* Truganini who had struck Yankee with clubs.[7]

The bodies were buried near a river mouth, probably that of Powlett River (named after Commissioner Powlett), east of Phillip Island. The whalers and miners then went with Anderson and Massie to their station to borrow a boat so they could sail up Westernport Bay to seek help from Lieutenant Rawson. The Massie and Anderson station was on the most southern part of the Bay, stretching past what is today the Anderson settlement at the turn-off to Phillip Island, right to the ocean. The boat was probably kept on the river, now known as Bass, that entered the Bay near their homestead.

All these places had long-established Aboriginal names, but most settlers had the habit of renaming all they saw, including renaming the Aborigines themselves.

La Trobe heard that trouble had started at Westernport before Massie's letter arrived. On Sunday evening, 4 October, a note was dropped at his door, telling him that Mr Jamieson, a station-holder of Westernport, was in town and wished to see him in the morning on a matter of urgency. A 'large party of Aborigines' had attacked his station and robbed it. He asked for help, since he expected to be attacked again.[8] La Trobe immediately decided that night to send troops and contacted Russell, Divisional Commander of the Mounted Police. Jamieson's station was a long way from Cape Patterson; it was due north of Lieutenant Rawson's base camp up towards Dandenong, near what today is Pakenham.

Several stations had been robbed by the Van Diemen's Land Aborigines before the two whalers were killed. They had raided station after station from Dandenong to Cape Patterson, walking thirty miles a day to avoid pursuit. Their tactics seemed to be to rob and burn down stations while avoiding unnecessary deaths and gun fights. They mainly stole fire-arms. They collected far more than they themselves could use. Whether they did this as their personal settler-disarmament campaign or for distribution to others, we do not know.

In those days, the country east of Melbourne was a continuous forest. The stations were merely huts in widely separated clearings.

The Tasmanians had begun, according to police reports,[9] by robbing Mr Horsefal of Dandenong of a fowling piece. (His station, although described as being at Dandenong, could be the 'Hosfolds' marked on Thomas's map as nearer Cranbourne.) They then moved on to Mr Ordon's. They laid siege to a building in which there were two men, firing several shots through the roof to try to set the building on fire. The men escaped by taking a plank from the back wall. 'The villains then crept down the chimney and stole 150 pounds of flour and a bag of sugar.'

Powlett and Rawson, immediately after hearing of the whalers' deaths, set out by boat to see if they could locate the killers. They both kept a written record of the events that followed.[10] Before dark, they hoped to reach Mr Mundy's station, about ten miles south from Rawson's hut near Settlement Point. Mundy, who was also at Rawson's at that time, offered to help by riding along the coast and lighting a fire on the cliff-top so they would know where to beach their small sailing boat.

There was no wind, so they had to row. Rawson and Powlett were accompanied by two policemen. Rawson tells what happened.

> We started and we pulled for about three hours without seeing any light. We fired several shots to give notice that we were near, but all to no purpose, and, after pulling till eleven o'clock, the tide having run out considerably, we were forced to land. The place where we landed was an open, reedy plain, not an ounce of wood within a mile of us. I had luckily put a bottle of brandy in the boat of which I gave a glass to all hands. We had no water and nothing to eat, so we had nothing to do but to lay down and go to sleep which we did after smoking our pipes. I slept soundly till morning, when I awoke stiff and cold, wet through with a heavy dew.[11]

Next day, 11 October, they finally made it to Mundy's station and made themselves some damper and tea. Mundy arrived as they finished eating. He had slept out as he couldn't find his way in the dark. They then travelled along the coast to Anderson's station where they heard that the Van Diemen's Land blacks had robbed several small stations nearby.

The Tasmanians Fight 65

Next morning, at four o'clock on a cold, wet, misty, miserable day, they loaded their guns and, taking with them three or four special constables sworn in for the occasion, went out to hunt down the blacks.

There were fourteen armed men in the party. Dividing themselves into two parties, they started combing their way through thick scrub up both sides of the nearby river where they suspected the blacks had hidden themselves. After five hours of searching, covered in scratches and soaked to the skin, the only things they had found were an abandoned double-barrelled shot-gun and a stomach pump!

They then decided that this was a waste of time. The only people who could track Aborigines in the bush were Aborigines. They would return to Melbourne and find themselves some black trackers.

So, on Wednesday 13 October, they set off by boat up Westernport Bay. On the way they decided to call in to see a Mr Westaway who was camped near the shore. Much to their surprise they found the Aboriginal group had been here as well. Without being seen, they had stripped all the contents from his tent, although it was in full view of Westaway and his men who were cutting timber nearby.

Rawson and Powlett could not stop to help as they would miss the tide. Just after they left, Westaway found where the Aborigines had hidden his possessions and recovered them, again without seeing the Aborigines. That night, sitting around their fire, the campers came under gunfire.

Mr Westaway and a companion bolted away from the dangerous light of the campfire into the bush. The Aborigines did not pursue them but raided the camp, taking from the tent firearms, a quality coat and most of £22 pounds in banknotes, which, according to Bob, Jack afterwards burnt. Meanwhile Rawson and Powlett were once again in trouble in their boat. They had delayed too long.

> Before we had gone five miles the tide went out and we were left high and dry on the mud flats where we were compelled to stop till the tide returned in six hours. It was bitterly cold, a high wind blowing and nothing to eat. We had luckily a cask of bottled ale in the boat which I was taking up to my station which we broached. What with the ale and continually smoking we managed to keep the life in us. At eight o'clock at night we floated. The wind having died away, we were forced to pull and reached my place at half past twelve after considerable difficulty in finding the river.[12]

They spent the next five days travelling to Melbourne, calling at many stations, 'putting them in a great state of alarm' with the news of the rebellious Tasmanians.

Melbourne was in a social whirl when they arrived back in town; Governor Gipps had come on an official visit. Rawson went down with him by coach to a public ball in Geelong.

Rawson or Powlett must have spoken to a journalist while they were in town for, in the newly-founded *Port Phillip Herald* on 29 October, appeared the first account of the raids by the Van Diemen's Land Aborigines.

> THE BLACKS: Information has been received in town that numerous depredations have been committed in the Westernport direction by a party of the Aborigines accompanied by and associated with two Van Diemen's Land blacks and three women who are as well skilled in the use of the firearms they possess as the males.
>
> These people had been imported by Mr Robinson for the purpose of aiding in the civilization of the Aborigines of Australia Felix.
>
> The daring party have extended their depredations to Dandenong and its vicinity, plundering Messrs Mundy's, Westaway's and different other stations and committing unmentionable atrocities... possessing a large quantity of firearms.

Powlett and Rawson left Melbourne that afternoon, again in the rain, and rode up to Dandenong. Here waiting for them were six policemen, six black trackers, a light cart and a tent. William Thomas, the Assistant Protector, was there too. He was going to travel with them, as was a Mr Ayse. Rawson commented that Thomas was 'a harmless inoffensive man, and, tho' living all his time in the bush, yet knew little of its ways.'

Remarkably, and very conveniently, the Van Diemen's Land Aborigines were not far away. They, too, had travelled to Dandenong, walking from Cape Patterson, and had raided a hut not far away. On the day after Rawson arrived at Dandenong, they stole a large quantity of ammunition from a Mr Allan. That same day, 30 October, Rawson and the others had set out once more to hunt them down, unaware this robbery had taken place. This time there were twelve on horseback followed by a cart full of supplies.

The Allan robbery prompted La Trobe to write to Robinson requesting him to 'go down immediately to the Dandenong district... to assist Crown Commissioner Powlett.' Robinson replied saying he would, but he never did leave to join the chase.[13]

The tracks of the Tasmanians were found by the black trackers, but cattle tracks had obscured them, perhaps by intent of the Van Diemen's Landers. In any case, the pursuers were soon lost. It seemed from the tracks they had found that the Tasmanians were heading back towards Westernport Bay, so they decided to head in that direction and to investigate a water-hole they might have used. The tracks were found again and were quite fresh. The military posse had been shooting kangaroos, then plentiful, as they moved through thickly-timbered country and storing them on the cart, but hunting was out now. They had to move quietly and quickly if they were going to be able to surprise the Tasmanians.

Suddenly a gun went off close to them. Someone was hunting nearby. The posse stole through the bush. The trackers found the spot where a man had stood a few minutes before shooting a kangaroo. But there was no sign of man or beast. They decided to leave the cart behind so they could move still more quietly. Two policemen stayed with the cart to protect it.

Soon they came across a new-dray track; on the track were the footprints of two Aborigines, the Van Diemen's Landers, going down the track towards the nearby station. Rawson recorded:

> It struck us that they might at that moment be robbing the station. We accordingly galloped down the road, we had not gone far, when I was astonished by Mr Protector Thomas (who had seldom been on horseback before) come flying past me without his hat, and a gun that he was carrying for some person entangled with his bridle, and looking the very picture of despair. Just as we came in sight of the station, we passed him again, lying on his back.[14]

When they got to the station, which belonged to a Mr Allen, they found the men there,

> getting their horses and arms ready to go in pursuit of the blacks, the place having been robbed about an hour previous to our arrival ... We found they [the Aborigines] had taken eight cannisters of powder, two guns and sundry pistols.

They decided to stop to eat, but two Aborigines came in saying that they had been shot at just a mile away while they were hunting kangaroo. They leapt on their horses, convinced it must be the Tasmanians, and raced off – only to find that they had been shot at by the police who were guarding the cart, for reportedly failing to stop!

That night the posse camped with two fires blazing and sentries posted. Protector Thomas once more got himself laughed at by the military who did their sentry duty sitting against trees well away from the firelight, their rifles on their knees. Thomas marched up and down in the moonlight, gun gleaming on his shoulder, holding himself as stiff as a rod. They told him he was an easy target for any Aborigine in the bush, but he considered there was infinitely more danger sitting down, so he kept on marching.

At one time during the night the party heard shots ringing out from a distance away. They considered going to see if a station were under attack, but remembered that some station owners had a habit of firing their guns at night just to warn off any nearby Aborigines.

Next day, Sunday 31 October, they went down to visit several nearby stations. They heard from one station that the Aborigines had turned up there and gave them the message that they would not be taken alive but would fight to the last. The police party recruited more people for the hunt. They now numbered eighteen mounted men and six on foot.

They found the tracks once more and moved off quietly into thick scrubby country. The tracks were quite fresh. The Tasmanians could be nearby. Rawson reported that the Aboriginal trackers were very nervous, showing

> evident signs of fear, and advancing with their guns full-cock – the three principal guides rejoiced in the names of – Mr Lively, Mr Langhorne and Pigeon, an old man dressed in a green frock coat . . . and a beaver hat, armed with an immense musket, and furthermore, to encourage him, I had lent him one of my pistols.
>
> We advanced this way about a mile and had arrived in sight of the sea, when bang went two guns close to us, and directly after we saw some people about 200 yards off. We were on a small thickly wooded hill. Immediately in front of us was an open flat, about 150 yards wide and then a thick scrub, in which we could see our opponents. Behind them was the sea.
>
> We dismounted and consulted how we should attack them. It was an awkward place for they could pick us off as we crossed the flat without our being able to see them. After reconnoitering, we determined to charge across. Accordingly, at a given signal, we started from out shelter into the flat, and immediately every horse was floundering up to its girths, the flat being a swamp.
>
> After a great deal of confusion and scrambling we all managed to get out again and, to our astonishment, without a

shot being fired at us – we now thought we would try the effect of a shot to see if it would bring them out, and Mr Hobson mounted into a tree with a rifle, and soon spied a fellow's head looking out from behind a bush, he immediately fired and the head disappeared. This not having the desired effect, we formed the party and started across on foot. On arriving close to the scrub, I summoned them to surrender, upon which they answered, if we would not fire they would come out. On coming out, to our astonishment, instead of five blacks, they were five whites, Mr Anderson and four servants out swan shooting, and it was Mr Anderson at whom Mr Hobson had fired. He had a lucky escape for the latter was a good shot and rarely missed.[15]

Fortunately, Anderson was sympathetic to their cause as he had been involved in the original discovery of the murdered whalers. He willingly agreed to join the party. Half an hour later they found that the Tasmanians had been cooking a meal nearby when they were alarmed by the gunfire. They had fled, leaving their fire still burning.

The posse quickly followed and, at midday, came in sight of them about three-quarters of a mile off, but once more the Aborigines escaped. Rawson described what happened.

We had a beautiful race, every horseman off as hard as he could go. But the villains took a swamp [sic] which the horses could not cross. We had to go a mile to a crossing place, and then return. We now lost all tracks for about an hour, the natives searching most patiently for about 2.00 p.m. [sic] One of them gave the signal, and away we went, the tracks leading for my station now about seven miles off with four creeks intervening about halfway there. The natives pointed out a smoke rising amongst the trees and at the same moment a dog barked. We galloped on, but the blacks were off. They had left almost everything. The bivouac was on the edge of an immense morass, in the middle of which we saw them, making for a thick scrub. Some horses refused to go in, and the others when they got in could not move. My pony was accustomed to it, having been in it often before. The water was about three feet deep with long reeds and soft bottom. We all worked away foot and horse, but could not get within shot before they reached the scrub, which was composed of tea tree, in which you could not see a yard either way. It was in the form of a triangle, each side about half a mile long. As soon as we had reconnoitred, we posted people at different places, and Mr Powlett took a party on one side, and Mr Hobson on the other and entered the scrub.

I took the place outside where I thought it was most likely they would come out with a rifle. Mr Foster stood in a lump of trees about fifty yards further off, with a horse pistol which would not have reached half way to the scrub.

Just before dark the parties came out of the scrub after an unsuccessful search. It was no use stopping as the place was too large to surround effectively after dark, besides it was anything but comfortable, standing so long in the water.[16]

It seems, from a report in the *Port Phillip Herald* on 9 November, that the Aborigines led their pursuers a merry dance by separating and whistling from different directions.

All the party had gained was a bit to eat and some stores. They eagerly ate up a damper that the Tasmanians had abandoned by their fire and took various stores that were also abandoned: flour, sugar, tea, gunpowder, caps, pocket compass, clothing. The damper wasn't much between so many so they returned to the station where they had left the cart, 'which we reached after dark, hungry, wet, tired and disappointed.'

Next morning, Monday 1 November, before setting out, Powlett took the opportunity to write an optimistic progress report to send La Trobe. 'I do not think much resistance will be made as they must have had several opportunities of firing upon us yesterday', he commented. He told La Trobe the natives had been out already that morning and found the tracks.

After he had finished his report the posse went to follow the tracks and found they seemed to lead towards the station of Lieutenant Rawson. They came to a river. Rawson thought they had crossed the river. Powlett disagreed. So they split up, Rawson crossing the river and going to his station, while Powlett continued searching up the river. On arrival at the station, Rawson found he was right: the Aborigines had been near his station that morning. They had been heard shooting game. So he sent for Powlett. The whole party slept on Rawson's floor that night.

Next day, tracks were impossible to find. A later report in the *Port Phillip Herald* said that 'the natives seized a whaleboat off Mr Anderson and put to sea',[17] but Rawson does not mention this. Possibly none of them knew of this at that time.

The Aboriginal trackers became exceedingly nervous. They feared for their lives at the hands of the Van Diemen's Landers.

They wanted a larger armed party to protect them if they were to continue.

Powlett decided to return to Melbourne on 2 November to seek more aid. The posse disbanded; Rawson stayed on at his station with two or three black trackers for several days, but he was apprehensive for there was evidence that the Van Diemen's Landers were still nearby. On 8 November he decided that he, too, would go back to Melbourne to get more armed support.

Meanwhile, Protector Thomas had gone with with two Aborigines to continue the search. They visited the now abandoned stations of Hawdon and Munday, then, on 5 November they came across the tracks of the hunted Tasmanians. Thomas immediately wrote to Robinson.

> I beg to inform you that this day we again came across the tracks of the Van Diemen's Land blacks about six or seven miles east by south of Mr Jamieson's. Your instructions were that I was to return unless I came across their tracks. As the blacks nor any other party was to make a move unless I or someone in authority is with them, it would be desirable that I do not return . . . the only way of capturing the parties will be at a station or by tracking, in which case more hands are needed, as stations have already been deserted and most of the parties fled to town. In consequence no casual assistance can be obtained now we have passed Mr Jamieson's station.
>
> There should be in my opinion at least twelve more blacks . . . and these dispatched immediately with equipment, clothing and rations.[18]

He asked for help to be sent to him at the place from which he wrote, Tobinnerk, where he had camped with blacks two years before. Next day, he wrote, he was going 'to proceed on the tracks which are no more than a day old.'

Six days later, from Old Settlement Hill many miles to the south, he pencilled an almost illegible desperate note to Robinson on a torn scrap of paper, not at all in his usual neat copperplate style.

> The policeman having to go to town, I avail myself of informing you we have the tracks to about one and a half miles from this spot . . . a calf they killed of Mr Anderson's . . . they have been, and I have every reason to believe are, the last three days in scrub about one and a half miles from here where I expect they will make a halt till their stores are out.
>
> Having but three blacks with me, I think it most prudent to let them remain where they are, till the remainder of the

blacks arrive. In fact, without more assistance in this scrubby part I think it impossible to take them. I . . . am now near Westaway's as the station most likely to be attacked again.

P.S. The blacks have behaved remarkably well, and watch in general and sortie for two or three hours every night. They are greatly in need of blankets. I trust you don't mind this being in pencil, the only means I have of addressing you.[19]

Robinson sent no help, but did complain about being addressed in pencil on torn paper despite Thomas's explanation. Thomas was to frostily explain that all the official notepaper supplied for the Assistant Protectors had been kept by Robinson for his own use!

The information Thomas had sent to town was very important for the hunters. The man whom Rawson had gently mocked as having no knowledge of the bush had succeeded, or rather his Aboriginal trackers had succeeded, in discovering the camping place of the Tasmanians, and in keeping it under surveillance unobserved.

Meanwhile, Rawson reached Melbourne in two days, arriving on 10 November, passing Mr Powlett on the road going to Arthurs Seat. He told Powlett the Van Diemen's Landers were still near his station and agreed to meet him on Friday 12 November at Dandenong. Powlett had received a report that the Aboriginal fighters had gone down to Cape Schanck and he was going to investigate. The report turned out to be false.

For the next two days in Melbourne, Rawson did all he could to get armed Aborigines to help him. But Superintendent La Trobe refused to arm any of the local Aborigines. He considered it too dangerous to make exceptions. He could not trust Aborigines with guns. Also, Rawson was refused help by nearly all the Aborigines camped by the Yarra. They would not help him track down the Tasmanian Aborigines. Robinson said he could find only six who would help. When Rawson went down to the camp, only one of the six agreed to go with him.

On Friday 12 November, Rawson travelled to Dandenong to meet up with Powlett as arranged. Here he received a message. The Van Diemen's Landers were attacking station after station down at Westernport. Rawson sent an urgent message to his commanding officer, Vignolles, for as many soldiers as he could spare. He asked for them to follow him to his station as soon as possible. They immediately set out for Westernport, recruiting from stations as they went. Thomas's report, locating the Van Diemen's Land Aborigines for them, had arrived. They intended to pounce as quickly as they could.

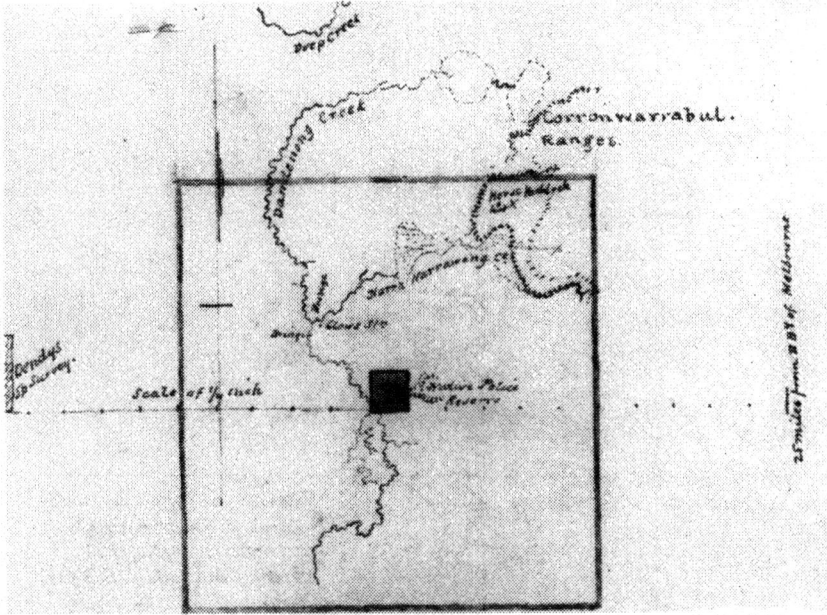

Location of the Native Police Reserve near Dandenong, *Public Record Office of Victoria*

Map showing where the main actions of this story took place. Based on sketch maps drawn by William Thomas

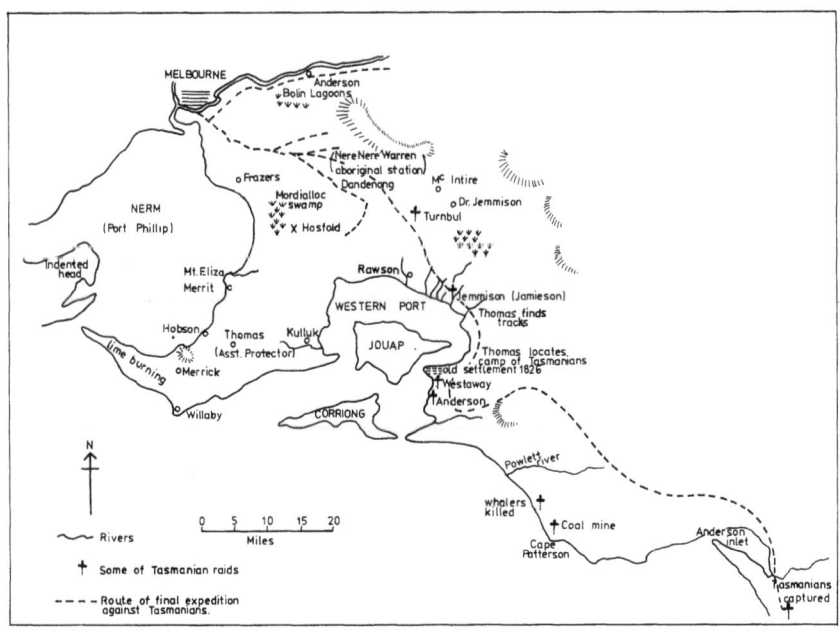

Journal of an
Expedition after some
Van Diemans Land Blacks
who were committing
depredations at Western
Port on the Southern
Coast of New Holland
October November 1841

Extract from Samuel Rawson's journal, in which he describes part of the chase, *National Library of Australia* (MS 2041)

October 8th Friday reached Western Port, my station, late at night
Octr 10th Mr Powlett, Commissioner Crown Lands, with two Police men arrived at about 5 oclock P.M. a large party, consisting of two coal miners wives & 4 whalers arrived from Massie & Anderson's in a boat with the intelligence of the murder of two of their party by some V.D.L. blacks who were at liberty in that neighbourhood the murder had taken place near Cape Patterson; but the blacks were supposed to be at Massie & Andersons. Mr Powlett and myself agreed immediately to start with the Police men in the boat — purposing to stay at Mr Mundy's station that night about 10 miles down the bay

Judge John Walpole Willis presided over the trial, *La Trobe Library, State Library of Victoria*

Order that sentence of death
may be carried into execution
on 2 Natives convicted of murder

// Colonial Secretary's Office
Sydney 5th January 1842

Sir

I am directed by His
Excellency the Governor to inform
you that in the cases of the
aboriginal natives named
Robert Timmy Jimmy Smallboy
and Jack Napoleon Timmy-
nimerpareney, Convicted at a
Criminal Session of the Supreme
Court holden at Melbourne,
of Murder, and sentenced to
suffer Death, the Sentence of the
Law is to be carried into
effect

His Honor
The Superintendent
of Port Phillip

Colonial Secretary's letter of 5 January 1842 authorising execution of Bob and Jack, *Public Records Office of Victoria*

By now all the squatters around Melbourne and Westernport were greatly alarmed and arming themselves to the teeth. Among these was Henry Meyrick, living on the Mornington Peninsula. It was at this time that he wrote to England saying that 'the whole neighbourhood has been thrown into the utmost confusion' by the Van Diemen's Land Aborigines. They had robbed Allen's station ten miles from his station, Colourt. 'Had they come on to Colourt we would have robbed the hangman of his fee for we had guns loaded enough to have annihilated a whole tribe.'

Not all chose to defend their stations, many of which, as Thomas had written, were by now deserted, their owners fleeing back to Melbourne.

Rawson and Powlett were joined by Anderson, an unnamed volunteer and two blacks. On 16 November, Corporal Jennings and eight more soldiers arrived. Powlett wrote a pessimistic report to La Trobe.

> If the blacks should continue in the scrub, I fear we shall have little chance of capturing them; no robberies have been committed since the one of Mr Allen's station but several cattle have been found shot on this and the adjoining run.[20]

On the 17th, they set off for Anderson's station about thirty-five or more miles away. Their hunting party was now made up by nine mounted police, nine soldiers, four black trackers, the white volunteer, Anderson, Powlett and Rawson – twenty-eight men all armed (including the Aborigines). One pack-horse carried all their food supplies. They hoped by riding light and fast they would soon surprise the Aborigines they pursued.

The country was very rough, thick scrub interspersed with bogs. They saw kangaroo, but dare not shoot for food for fear of alarming the Van Diemen's Land blacks. It rained for hours; they were exhausted and drenched when they decided to stop at Westaway's camp, four miles short of Anderson's station. There, waiting for them, was Protector William Thomas with two Aborigines. He had grim news to tell Anderson. His station had been robbed that day and one of his men seriously wounded by a bullet in the chest. This raid was typical of those made by the Tasmanian fighters.

The *Port Phillip Herald* had a full report.

> The fellows arrived at Anderson's station at about 3.00 p.m. and watched the men leave the house after their dinner. They then entered the house to find there two women and a child.

They first turned the two women out of the house and Jack stood sentry over them. Bob then robbed the premises of three fowling pieces, three bags of shot and a quantity of flour and sugar.[21]

Jack reassured one of the women when she began to cry for fear the child would be harmed. They would not harm women or children. Everywhere they went, they concentrated on taking all the weapons they could find, and the supplies they needed. But sometimes they burnt the stations after robbing them, perhaps to drive the settlers from the bush.

Next day Anderson and the others scouted around his station. They followed track after track but all proved false. It was not till dusk that they found the right track. They set out at first light next morning. There were now twenty-nine of them, all males, on horseback in pursuit of five, well-armed Aborigines on foot, two men and three women.

The track led at first towards the coal mine at Cape Patterson which was only four miles along the coast from Anderson's. But soon the tracks went up to the top of the South Gippsland hills. Here the Europeans had a rest. 'We laid down and enjoyed the magnificent view. From the height we were, we could see the whole of Western Port.' It was some time until the black trackers located the track down the hill. It was a steep scramble down through thick scrub. At the foot they discovered a creek. They had no water with them now – thirstily, they rushed to get a drink. But it was too brackish. A mile further on another creek proved drinkable but not too pleasant. Here they discovered the Tasmanians' camp of two nights previous.

They rested again. 'The weather very hot so we laid down and smoked our pipes while our blacks performed a great many ceremonies to show that the expedition was to be successful.'

They went on a few miles further and found the Tasmanians' previous night's camp. They were not moving quickly. Perhaps they were not aware of the closeness of the pursuit. Here they abandoned a single-barrel gun, some women's clothing and a bundle of potatoes. The latter were a very welcome find as the hunting party had run out of food. They thought the signs were that the blacks were getting tired. The Aborigines had travelled for days, keeping ahead of mounted men. About four miles further on, they came across a fire still burning, and found a bullet and the remains of some lead, where the Aborigines had been casting bullets.

The hunting party cautiously moved on through open forest. They heard a shot fired – the Tasmanians were hunting for food. They crept forward and came out on the side of a creek running into the sea through a range of sandhills.

The creek was some forty feet wide where they were to cross and the sandhills on the far side of it separated them from the sea. It was some thirty miles beyond Powlett River, according to Rawson, so it was, most likely, the river now known as the Tarwin at Venus Bay. The dunes here back a long, straight beach along which one can see for miles, as could Rawson. There is a lagoon behind the dunes, some five miles south of the river crossing-place, as Rawson is to describe. If indeed it was the Tarwin, they must have crossed upstream of its wide, shallow mouth.

There was a good chance that the blacks were out on the sands hunting for shellfish which was a popular source of food, especially for Van Diemen's Land Aborigines.

> While some went by the creek, some of us went to the top of the hills, but the beach was all clear for some miles. It was now near four o'clock, so we halted and lighted a fire to roast our potatoes, as we could not do it after dark on account of it being seen. We had one potato each, which we enjoyed exceedingly, and then commenced our march.[22]

They crossed the creek and pushed forward as fast as they could, trying to catch up with the Tasmanians before dark, but they could not. Four miles past the creek, they called a halt and made a cold, fireless camp. They were not feeling at all optimistic. Rawson described their camp.

> We encamped, that is to say, we laid down. Our tobacco was nearly finished, we having only about half a pipe full each, and nothing to eat, and only cold water to drink. No fire, a cold night, and having the same distance to go back that we had come before we could get anything, without [having] captured the blacks, anything but pleasant.[23]

They sent on the black trackers after dark to see if they could spot the Aboriginal camp.

> About 9.00 p.m. they returned, and to our great joy said they had seen their fire about a mile off, so Mr Powlett and I immediately arranged our plans to march just before daylight, so as to come upon them at sunrise in hope of surprising them as blacks generally sleep late into the morning. Mr Thomas wanted to go forward to negotiate with them, he being a man

of peace, but that we would not allow. After we had arranged this, we laid down and slept.

SATURDAY NOVEMBER 20TH. Arose about 4.00 a.m., a cold morning, heavy dew falling. Having examined our arms to see that all was right, we marched in silence in single file, the blacks leading to point out the way, which lay under a range of sand hills about half a mile from the sea. After advancing half a mile we had to cross a lagoon, water two feet deep, anything but pleasant on a cold morning with an empty stomach. We advanced some time, till we began to think the guides had lost the tracks, when just as the sun was rising, they pointed out the smoke of the fire, rising above a few shrubs, about twenty or thirty yards below us. We were on a sand hill, at the bottom of which was the camp and immediately beyond that was a thick scrub, almost impassable for a black man, and quite so for a white man, and as they had dogs with them, I was afraid of their giving the alarm and giving them an opportunity of hiding in the scrub. I extended the men along the top of the hill, and then myself in the centre advanced in a kind of semicircle down upon them. Each man was six feet apart, with orders to take them alive if possible, but if they offered resistance or to escape to shoot them at once.

Here Rawson's account differs from the account officially presented by Powlett and reported in the Port Phillip papers. Powlett's account seems to have been sanitized for official purposes. His report to La Trobe stated: 'On our approaching the camp site, the two men Bob and Jack got into the scrub. Several shots were fired at Jack and one slightly grazed the woman who was making off.' The *Port Phillip Herald* of 26 November 1841 reported, 'They fired a shot over their heads. They all rushed into the scrub but were still surrounded and several shots were fired at Jack.'

Rawson's journal paints a far more vivid picture. He talks of a murderous volley that the Aborigines were lucky to survive.

We advanced down the hill, and were closing in upon them, I was about six feet from the fire, and could see them laying down, when a policeman who was on my left, catching a glimpse of a man's head, without orders, fired and missed him. He was rather behind me at the time, that I was not certain from which party the shot came – Immediately out rushed dogs and men, the first at us, the latter to the scrub, every body fired at them as they got a sight of them. I fired both barrels, right and left, and I saw one drop. I had five pistol balls in each barrel. I immediately ordered the men to surround the scrub to prevent their escape, and then I went to reconnoitre the camp and find out the state of their larder, as, tho' I had ordered the scrub to be surrounded in case of accidents, yet from the heavy fire opened upon them, I concluded they must be all shot. While I was turning over the blankets with the end of my gun, I discovered a woman. I handed her over to a policeman to put handcuffs on her and a little further I discovered another. After they were secured, I put a pistol to their heads and told [them] to call their companions out of the scrub if they were alive.

In his diary Samuel Rawson claimed he drew the only Aboriginal blood of this attack.

In about a minute out came a woman covered in blood from a wound in the head, a ball had struck the back of the head and cut the scalp open without injuring the skull, and from the size of the wound, was caused by a small ball and was the one that dropped when I fired. Just now a man was taken escaping from the other side of the scrub, and directly after, we saw the other haring across the country near half a mile off – we told the women to call him back – and on our promising not to shoot him, he came back and was secured. We thus had the whole party and to our astonishment only one wounded, which was owing to the thickness of the underwood, tho' it must have been sharp work, as about thirty balls were sent at their heads.

All the captives were secured with hand-cuffs on their wrists and with chains on their legs.

As soon as this was done, we examined the camp and found six or seven double and single guns – and pistols, also a large supply of ammunition – about 60 pounds of flour and the same quantity of sugar, several pounds of tobacco and a number of cloaks and blankets.

A copper bullet mould, 'capable of casting fifty balls at a time', was also found. One of the four pistols found was equipped with a spring bayonet.[24] The pistols and rifles were later all found to be stolen from a Mr Mercer. Then, Rawson wrote, the ravenous police and soldiers proceeded to have a meal from the captured stores.

A man was immediately set to work to make some cakes of the flour and in half an hour each man was supplied with cake and water from the swamp *ad libitum*. As soon as breakfast was over, we prepared for a start – Mr Powlett took three of the prisoners and the Police about thirty miles further on to examine the place the where two men had been murdered, while I with the soldiers and the other prisoners returned. The day was very hot and after a very severe march we reached Mr Anderson's station at 3.00 p.m. where we were received with great joy, the women crying and looking upon us as their deliverers and ready to do anything in the world for us.[25]

Meanwhile, Mr Powlett took three of the prisoners, Truganini, Jack and Bob, to the place where the whalers had been killed, some thirty miles away. Truganini acted as a guide, showing where the whalers were buried.*

The Aboriginal prisoners, once they had recovered from the initial shock, 'seemed to treat the whole affair with great levity and to answer freely and openly every question',[26] according to the report of one of the policemen.

However, conflicting stories were told about the killing. According to Corporal Johnson, an Aboriginal tracker in the Border Police, Bob said that Jack fired the first shot killing one whaler instantly and that Jack threatened then to shoot Bob unless he shot at the other whaler. Johnson added that Bob, after making this statement, pretended he could not speak English and made signs with his hands as if to indicate he beat Yankee around the head.[27] If he was pretending not to speak English, it is hard to see how Bob made the confession.

At his trial Bob was to claim that Truganini and Jack beat Yankee around the head. According to a policeman's statement published in the *Port Phillip Herald* of 26 November, Truganini, after her capture, freely admitted that she had hit Yankee about the head. But Corporal Johnson said at the trial that Truganini had told him at the time, after visiting the grave, that one of the men had cudgelled Yankee's head. Johnson said he was told that all the women were together at the time of the killing, standing terrified and crying up on the sand hill watching the killing on the beach.

Powlett returned with the prisoners before dark. After a day's rest at Anderson's they started on their way back, the prisoners being sent off with the troopers. Powlett and Rawson once more

---

* The Aboriginal trackers were to get a reward of a blanket each for their essential role in the capture of the Tasmanians, and this only because Thomas insisted on some reward for them

decided to take the easy way back by going by boat instead of forcing their way through the bush. However, once again, unbelievably, they ran into trouble. 'The wind being very light, we only got to Mr Mundy's deserted station. The boat grounded some distance from shore about 11.00 p.m. and we had to wade for it.'[28] After camping out, they made it to Rawson's station in time to have breakfast before the prisoners arrived.

The Aboriginal prisoners finally arrived in Melbourne on 26 November 1841, in chains and under a military escort. The Van Diemen's Land Aborigines' armed fight against the invaders who took their land, a struggle that had lasted thirty-seven years, had ended.*

---

* There are reports that some Aborigines were still on the Tasmanian mainland and robbing whites; a family were captured late 1842.

Chapter Seven
The Trial

The Van Diemen's Land Aborigines were sent to trial before a jury and Melbourne's first Supreme Court Judge, the notorious Mr Justice Willis. Willis had previously served in Canada and British Guinea and been forced out of office in both places. Sent to Sydney in 1837, he feuded with the Chief Justice, attending his judgements where he made loud asides questioning the Chief Justice's competence. In 1841 he was transferred once more, this time to Melbourne, where he finally ended his career becoming, some say, the only judge in British history to be twice removed from the High Bench.[1]

On Aboriginal issues he was especially controversial. Governor Gipps labelled him, after his final removal in 1843, an 'apologist for the cruellest practices by some of the least respectable of the settlers on the Aborigines.[2]

Yet some of his judgements deeply upset the authorities because they recognized the right of Aborigines to rule their own affairs. He questioned the whole basis of the British assumption of authority over Aborigines in a judgement of great significance and relevance today.

An Aborigine called Bonjon came before him in September 1841 charged with having killed a fellow Aborigine. Of the 200 arrested on the Yarra bank in October 1840, Bonjon was the only one still held. His defence council argued that Port Phillip, having 'become appended to the British Crown by occupancy, and no treaty had been entered into by the natives, they were not subjects, nor had they submitted themselves to the British Crown.[3]

Willis, presiding in the one story brick cottage on the south-east corner of King and Bourke Streets, that served as the Supreme Court for six-year-old Melbourne, said in his judgement:

Aborigines cannot be considered as foreigners in a kingdom which is their own.

I repeat, I am not aware of any express enactment or treaty subjecting the Aborigines of this colony to the English Colonial law.

Aborigines must be dealt with as distinct, though dependent, tribes governed among themselves by their own rude laws and customs. If this is so, I strongly doubt the propriety of my assuming the exercise of jurisdiction in the case before me.[4]

He knew the colonial authorities would not like his judgement. But he asked, 'Why, if this principle has been acknowledged ... regarding the Aborigines of New Zealand, [and elsewhere] why is it not to be acted on here?'

He quoted numerous examples where native law continued, despite British conquest, with the agreement of British authorities: in the East Indies, Ireland, New Zealand etc. He ruled that Aboriginal law had legal force still in Australia, at least concerning crimes inflicted by Aborigines on Aborigines. 'It is evident they have laws and usages of their own and they are not inconsiderate in number.'

It could not be said, he ruled, that the Aborigines had been conquered, as they received the British in a friendly way; nor could it be said, he added, that they ceded their rights by treaty. But, he continued, a nation could take another nation's land if the latter 'had too much of it for their own needs', and the former nation had a greater need. He decided Aborigines had no right to more than they could settle and cultivate. He did not consider the needs of a hunter gatherer economy. To him it was plain. They had more land than they needed and Britain had a greater need. Thus he justified the British settling in Australia.

He did not see this as extinguishing Aboriginal land-ownership rights or compelling expropriation by force. He praised the Quakers for purchasing the land they settled on in North America from the Indians, thus recognizing the land ownership rights of the prior inhabitants.

Willis finally ruled that he had no right to pass sentence on an Aborigine for an act committed among Aborigines. He set Bonjon free. This brought an immediate and furious response from the Sydney authorities who held that Aborigines were subject to British law by declaration of the British! If they had upheld Willis's ruling, then they would have had to halt the wholesale dispossession of the tribes.

However, when a white man, Bolden, was arraigned before Willis on a charge of killing Takier, an Aborigine, he directed the jury to acquit. He maintained that he had jurisdiction in this case as it was white against black, not black against black. He said that in such a case, Aborigines were entitled to be considered with the same rights as British citizens.[5]

George Bolden held Leighton Station which was on the Hopkins River in the Western District. Nearby, there was a run established for Aborigines by Protector Sievwright. Bolden was accused of attacking with whips an Aboriginal man, woman and child crossing his station on the way to the Aboriginal station.

In self-defence, the Aboriginal man attempted to pull Bolden from his horse. Bolden was accused of shooting him in the stomach and then killing him with a second shot when he tried to escape into a waterhole. The woman was killed with blows to the head; the boy escaped and told Sievwright what had happened. Willis refused to accept the boy's evidence, the evidence of an Aborigine.

Willis ruled that a leaseholder has the right 'to turn off by all lawful means any person whether white or black who should trespass on his run.'[6] At that time, much was made of Bolden being a close friend of the judge. Willis described Bolden to the jury as 'the brother of a near and respected neighbour of mine.'

La Trobe questioned this judgement in a letter to the Governor, for there was manifest inhumanity in refusing Aborigines access to their tribal lands. He said this legal ruling could cause much violence between Aborigine and white.[7]

But the settlers from the first had claimed the right to expel Aborigines from their pastoral leases. La Trobe himself had repeatedly sought to ban Aborigines from Melbourne. The British authorities were responsible, not Willis, for making no legal provision in the leases to protect Aboriginal access rights to tribal lands.

No white person was convicted in Melbourne for killing Aborigines until 1848, and the sentence then was only two months' gaol. By then, five Aborigines had been executed in Melbourne for killing whites. Aborigines were far from equal in the law. The non-acceptance of Aboriginal evidence made it nearly impossible for them to seek redress in the colonial courts: they could not lay charges nor testify. Only if there was a sympathetic white witness could any prosecution have the slightest hope of success.

Usually in such cases, the only white witness present would be the person or persons accused by the Aborigines of committing the crime. Therefore only the evidence of the accused would be accepted. The ruling against Aboriginal evidence conveniently protected the squatters from accusations of genocide.

The ruling also meant that whenever Aborigines were accused of crimes against whites, as in the case of the Van Diemen's Land Aborigines', they could *not speak in their own defence, produce an alibi or call Aboriginal witnesses.*

In 1838 there were moves to slightly improve this situation by allowing Aboriginal evidence – if it was corroborated by circumstantial facts or by the testimony of whites! A Bill was passed to make this the law, but the British disallowed it, following the advice of the Attorney-General and Solicitor-General, Campbell and Wilde respectively, that 'to admit in a criminal case the evidence of a witness acknowledging to be ignorant of God or a future state, would be contrary to the principles of British Jurisprudence'.![8]

In 1843 moves to legally recognize Aborigines in British courts met with a very hostile reception in Australia. Charles Wentworth, 'the Father of Australian Democracy', argued that Aborigines were scarcely human. 'It would *be quite as defensible to receive as evidence in a Court of Justice the chatterings of the orang-outang as of this savage race.*'[9]

In 1849 Aboriginal recognition in court was again rejected on the grounds that conflict was inevitable and the two races should be allowed to fight it out. Wentworth on this occasion advocated the use of the military against the tribes.[10]

When Jack, Bob, Fanny, Matilda and Truganini came up before Willis on 20 December 1841, they came under a legal system with mandatory heavy sentences. In the previous case before this court, a Patrick Kelly had been sentenced to transportation for life* for the offence of horse-stealing.[11]

There were two alternative charges brought against the Aborigines. By the first, Robert (Bob) Smallboy was the principal defendant. He was charged with shooting and killing; the others were charged with aiding and abetting. Alternatively, all of them were charged with murder.

Mr Redmond Barry, the standing Defence Council for Aborigines, who, later, as Chief Justice was to sentence Ned Kelly to

---

* This was a singularly inappropriate sentence in Australia, but the judge had to administer British laws with British prescribed sentences. In Melbourne, transportation was interpreted to mean moving the convicted to Tasmania or other parts of the colonies. Victorian Aborigines were sentenced to transportation to other states for raiding sheep stations.

death, tried to get a jury who might be more sympathetic to his clients. He argued that as they were not naturalized subjects of the Queen, they were entitled in natural justice to a jury made up half of 'aliens' – people not subjects of the Queen.[12] The judge would not allow this. Even if he had, Aborigines could not have sat on the jury, even as aliens, since they had less legal rights than any alien.

The Crown Prosecutor then said he wanted to drop the charge of murder, as one of his major witnesses was absent. Samuel Evans, one of the whalers, had not arrived in town. Evans may have been witness to people, running to the scene of the murder, who were possibly the Aborigines.

In this case, the refusal of the courts to recognize the validity of Aboriginal evidence could have worked in favour of the blacks. The only direct evidence was the confessions of the Aborigines themselves. However, this was not going to be allowed to stand in the way of punishing blacks for killing whites. British law can be infinitely adaptable.

Willis said the murder charges should stand as he did not want (black) murderers to escape the cause of justice. He accepted the statement by Truganini accusing Bob and Jack of the murder, thereby giving her an 'honorary white' status.

Once more, Barry, the Defence Council, questioned the whole legal basis of British authority over Aborigines. He argued the issue on the basis of natural justice and emotional sympathy.

It must be remembered that these people and fellow countrymen once roamed the green hills and wide plains of their native land, the lords of all around, subject to no will but their own, no master but their own passions.

[We must remember] the course of their destruction, at first insidious and private, then open and declared, which eventually swept a numerous nation off the face of their native country and transported the remnant to a foreign to them, distant shore. Before the termination of the war, the Government stated in a Dispatch that the first aggression – had been committed by the whites.

Barry asked how could Aborigines 'forget quietly what had happened? The whole feelings of the wild and untutored savage must predominate. Revenge in minds like theirs was not easily forgotten.'[13] He said that the evidence was very dubious and circumstantial. The confessions were clearly from a people in a state of terror and could not be relied on. It was already conceded that there was little evidence apart from Aboriginal confessions and circumstantial facts. There were no white witnesses to the killings.

He particularly argued for the Van Diemen's Land women because of the 'slavish subjection of the women to the men'. No direct evidence was brought up on this point, which could have been a ploy to try to save at least the women from the hangman's noose.

Powlett gave evidence that one of the Aboriginal women, Truganini, had, without either threats or solicitations on his part, described how the men, and the men alone, had killed the whalers. In collaboration he produced the 'bloody bludgeon'. Her evidence was greatly stressed in the trial. Bob's testimony that she had taken part was disregarded. So too was the evidence of a mounted policeman, reported in the papers, that Truganini initially confessed to helping the two men kill the sealers.

Powlett said that, at the time, 'they accused each other of firing the first shot.' Nonetheless, Powlett, stated in court that he believed it was definitely Jack, the reputed leader of the group. The *Port Philip Herald*, on 26 November, said Jack had admitted firing the first shot. In court, however, Jack remained silent. He incriminated none of the others, unlike Truganini and Bob who seem to have tried to shift the blame. Powlett added that Yankee could have been clubbed by more than one person, as four sticks were found near the bodies. The other women, Matilda and Fanny, made no confession of note.

Robert Robins, one of the whaling party, testified to what he saw after he heard two shots at the mining camp.

> I saw four people on the hill near the hut, I could not distinguish their colour ... one minute after the shots were fired three of the four went down to the beach and one stopped on the hill. I did not see a gun in the hands of the person who stopped on the hill. I saw two guns in the hands of some of the party before they came down. I could not see the beach they went to.[14]

Watson gave evidence of what Truganini stated at the time she took them to the shared grave. 'Truganini said she had stood on the high bank when the men were killed. She hid herself behind a bush with the other women as she was scared when she saw a man wounded and struggling on the sand.'[15]

This seems to be inconsistent with Robert Robins's evidence. Who was the third person who ran down to the beach? If Robins was right, his evidence would tie in with that of the mounted policeman reported in the *Port Phillip Herald* who said that three took part in the killing and that 'Truckannini' had confessed her part. If this is so, then Truganini was swift to change her story before she spoke to Watson.

Robins's evidence was also consistent with Bob's confession. Watson said that Bob confessed at that time to firing the second shot that hit Yankee. He said Jack had fired first and then compelled him at gun-point to fire. He said that Truganini and Jack had finished Yankee off with clubs.

Watson's evidence on what Truganini had said was accepted by the jury and, with it, the statement made by Truganini that she was innocent. Bob's evidence was disregarded. As Aborigines, neither Truganini nor Bob, could be called to the stand for cross-examination.

Robinson gave evidence for the good character of the Aborigines whom he had known for thirteen years. He spoke particularly well of Jack, 'brought up by him since his childhood and who had accompanied him in all his journeys in Van Diemen's Land.' Jack had also been of great use to him on his recent tour to the west. He left Mr Robinson ostensibly to go to the Protectorate Station under Mr Thomas. He had not been heard of since, 'until named as the ringleader in the outrages at Western Port.' He said his conduct had always been 'exemplary'.[16]

Robinson said the others had also always conducted themselves 'in the most exemplary manner'. He spoke of how Bob had gone to Adelaide as a servant of Langhorne and Bacchus and how Langhorne owed his life to him after Bob defended him from the attack of Aborigines along the Murray. 'I never knew him dishonest and he was always industrious.' He praised Truganini too, and told how she had saved his life in Tasmania. 'I am indebted to that woman for the preservation of my life on one occasion at Arthurs River. I have never found these persons wanting in humanity.'

The other two women, Matilda and Fanny, he said he had 'emancipated from the sealers'. He commented that 'The women act in great awe of the men. They are not allowed by the men to act according to their own will, they are in absolute thralldom.'[17] This was to be decisive evidence in the jury's eyes, although of dubious validity. It helped save the women's lives.'

The *Port Phillip Herald* of 21 January 1842 was to report that Bob later 'confessed that he was instigated to commit the crime by the native women in revenge for the killing of their friends at Port Arthur.'[18]

Robinson also gave evidence that the accused understood the principles of religion and knew right from wrong. This was of importance in establishing the legal validity of Truganini's confession.

In his final address to the jury and to the packed court-house, Judge Willis compared this case to that of Bonjon. He said Bonjon was not accused of killing a white but an Aborigine. He quoted Governor Gipps.

As human beings partaking of one common nature but less enlightened than ourselves – as the original possessors of the soil from which the wealth of the colony has been principally derived and as subjects of the Queen whose sovereignty extends over every part of New Holland, the Natives of the whole territory have the acknowledged right to the sympathy and kindness of every separate individual. *In disputes among themselves they may be governed by their ancient usages, wherever these do not interfere with the rights and safety of their more civilised fellow subjects.*

In disputes between the Aborigines and the whites, both parties are equally entitled to demand the protection and the assistance of the law of England. To allow either to injure or oppress the other, and still more to permit the stronger to regard the weaker party as aliens with whom a war can exist, and against whom they may exercise belligerent rights, is not less inconsistent with the spirit of that law, than it is at variance with the dictates of justice and humanity.[19]
(Emphasis as in newspaper account.)

Willis said that he believed that if the Aborigines could be persuaded to remain on reserves set aside for them, these unfortunate events might never have occurred. He saw this now as the only remedy. In his final words, the judge recommended the jury to bear the following in mind.

There is duty that you owe to yourselves and to your fellow subjects, to protect not only their property, but more especially their lives, and by your verdict to prevent if possible (should you deem the prisoners or any of them to have been actors in them), the recurrence of similar acts of aggression.[20]

Late on Monday night, 20 December 1841, the jury took just half an hour to come to their decision. They found the two men guilty of murder and acquitted the women totally. They added to their judgement a very strong plea for clemency 'on account of general good character and the peculiar circumstances under which they are placed.'

Next day the five returned to court for sentencing. Judge Willis first discharged the women into the care of Robinson with the fervent hope that they might be confined to Robinson's house and not allowed out. He then donned his black cap. Addressing the accused men, he said:

> Prisoners at the bar, you have been convicted by a jury of colonists of the murder of the whalers ... by the confession of Bob and the statement of Truganini there can be no doubt of your guilt ... the punishment that awaits you is not one of vengeance but of terror ... to deter similar transgressions ... you will be taken to the place of execution and severally be hanged by the neck until dead.[21]

When Willis forwarded his verdict to Gipps he made it obvious that he did not support the plea for clemency.[22] La Trobe also would not support it. Willis considered recommending that the execution be held out in the bush near the site of the crime in order to maximize the deterrent value to the tribes of the area, but this idea was abandoned as impractical. He also wanted an Aboriginal hangman.

The *Port Phillip Herald*, in its editorial of Christmas Eve 1841, expressed the strong feeling of many against any clemency and against the whole system of Protectors.

> The oft-repeated and, in certain circles, the so-popular argument of pseudo-philanthropists that the soul is the property of the blacks, and therefore the laws of nature force them to resist invasion on the part of the whites, cannot be advanced as ... an excuse.
>
> They are Aborigines of a different country, in no way connected with the New Hollanders, either by previous intercourse, similarity of laws, language or custom. [Mercy will encourage] their more-savage brethren in their career of blood and plunder and the whites will reasonably infer that whilst the blacks have their protectors, they have no security against their crimes. [Here the paper was referring to the one and only hanging of whites for killing blacks – the Sydney Myall Creek case.]
>
> Whilst the laws protect the blacks, the white man's blood must remain unavenged.[23]

The *Port Phillip Gazette* editorialized that this trial established the Aboriginal 'ineradicable love of destruction and, as a consequence, the *imperative necessity of coercion in their management.*'[24]

Melbourne's first Supreme Court, south-west corner of Bourke and King Streets, W. F. E. Liardet, *La Trobe Library, State Library of Victoria*

Bob and Jack being drawn to gallows hill, W. F. E. Liardet, *La Trobe Library, State Library of Victoria*

Truganini in her later years, H. H. Baily photograph, *Tasmanian Museum and Art Galley*

Cape Barren Island school children, January 1911. Clearly Truganini was not the last of the Tasmanians. *State Library of Tasmania*

A family of Aborigines at the Lake Tyers settlement, 1860s, *La Trobe Library, State Library of Victoria*

Tasmanian Aborigines, taken around 1900

However, the *Gazette* concluded by recommending mercy. 'They have been late from the boundless enjoyment of a life free as the woods and waters of their rugged clime, they have pined like prisoned eagles.' Instead of the death sentence, it recommended they should be sent for life to 'the prisons of Cockatoo Island'.[25] But the *Gazette* dropped its plea for mercy before the time came for the execution.

*

A FINAL MYSTERY. This account has had to be assembled solely from the recollections of those white people who were most involved. Many questions remained unanswered because, as previously stated, the Aborigines were not allowed to speak in their own defence, to be cross-questioned in court, or call Aboriginal witnesses.

A recently-discovered letter suggests that some key evidence, sent by Protector William Thomas to La Trobe on 21 July 1843, may be missing.

> But the recollection that had one of my former reports gone faithfully up to the Government (which was sent back to me with severe reproof) those two unfortunate Aborigines who suffered at Melbourne might still have been in existence.[26]

What was in his report is still unknown.

Chapter Eight
The Execution

Despite their conviction, Bob and Jack had high hopes of a reprieve because of the jury's recommendation of mercy and Robinson's support. The *Port Phillip Patriot* of 18 January reported that initially they were so sure of a reprieve that they were often 'laughing... losing none of their buoyancy of spirits.' They frequently played in the prison yard, using a bundle of rags as a substitute for a ball. This was despite the dreadfully overcrowded conditions in the Eastern Watch-house, where over seventy prisoners were confined in four filthy, vermin-ridden cells.

However, to their horror, and to the surprise of many, the plea for mercy was rejected by the Executive Council of New South Wales. The *Gazette* reported on 19 January 1842:

> EXECUTION OF THE BLACKS. Tomorrow the last vengeance of the law is to be carried into effect against the guilty natives of Van Diemen's Land whose outrages and trial before the Supreme Court, have occupied, during the progress of events, so much public attention.
>
> The two men who were brought as guilty will be hung at the site of the new gaol building on the hill which runs parallel with the north line of La Trobe Street. Their sentence will be carried out at seven o'clock in the morning and thus will close the last scene of their tragic and exciting history.

Most of the colonial papers had campaigned for the execution of the Aborigines. One of the exceptions was the *Gazette*. The above report continued to comment on the recent pardoning of whites who killed blacks and deplored that 'the same authority that shows mercy to whites who kill Aborigines, shows no mercy to Aborigines who kill whites.'

The papers monitored what was happening with great interest; there had never been an execution in Melbourne before. They reported that Bob in his last few days was very cast down and careworn and that he rejected food and tobacco on his last night. When Robinson visited, Bob showed his feelings and wept.

Jack, on the other hand, was a man apparently at peace with the world. He appeared most of the time in good spirits, eating half a loaf and drinking three pannikins of tea on his last night. He had his pipe of tobacco and offered it to Bob, who rejected it. When Robinson visited he was self-contained and quiet.

Reverend Thomson remained with them most of the evening and stayed until 2.00 a.m. He reported to the journalists that both had been very serious when he was with them and attentive to the prayers. At about 4.30 a.m., after two hours of sleep, they had breakfast. Jack ate 3 lbs (1.4 kg) of bread and two pannikins of tea; Bob only had a little tea when pressed. Jack then smoked his pipe. When shaved and dressed, Jack was gay. He laughed heartily when helped on with the long, white socks provided by the government. The gaoler remembered that Jack said he would join his father in Van Diemen's Land after his death and hunt kangaroo. He said he had three heads, one for the scaffold, one for the grave and one for Van Diemen's Land.

Bob however remained totally quiet.

Robinson arrived early, just after breakfast, bringing with him Truganini's stepson, Peter Brune, to make his farewell. Robinson was horrified to see the suit of white clothes the authorities had provided for them, white cap, shirt, trousers and stockings, with a white cape over all. He reported; 'Mr Orton wept and disapproved of dressing up the victims. Jack first put them on. Bob refused but was prevailed upon. I was much affected.'[1]

A journalist wrote that the contrast of the white clothes 'with their nearly jet-black hands and faces gave the criminals an appearance particularly revolting.'[2]

Reverend Thomson returned at 7.00 a.m. with the sheriff and several magistrates. All the prisoners attended Divine Service in the yard. Then Bob and Jack got up into Robinson's new cart drawn by two grey horses. A cover had been put up to shield them from public view. They were taken by a roundabout route through the city, along Collins, William and Lonsdale Streets, north up Swanston Street, then east into La Trobe Street, past the new public library into the execution site opposite, where the gallows grimly stood. Robinson did not go to the gallows but instead went to the burial ground to await their bodies.

The gallows stood on a small rise east of Swanston Street and north of La Trobe Street, the site now occupied by the Royal Melbourne Institute of Technology. To the east of the scaffold were the partly-built walls of the controversial New Melbourne Gaol (now Old Melbourne Gaol) and the treadmill, both then under construction. La Trobe Street was effectively the northern border of the settlement and the site of the execution was only partly cleared with several trees remaining.

The executioner was not an Aborigine as Willis had wanted. He was a convict by the name of John Davies. He had been sentenced to life transportation in the Chester Assizes, England, for the crime of sheep-stealing. It was his first offence. He had to leave behind him his wife and two daughters. He had been promised his freedom and ten pounds if he were to act as executioner.[3]

Eighteen convicts competed for the post of Public Executioner. Some convicts wanted more than the offered terms. They asked Robinson if the heads of the Aborigines could be had after the execution.[4] There was much demand for Aboriginal skulls and skeletons from ethnologists in England who believed they were a missing link in the evolution of humankind. Their skulls would thus attract a good price. The request was refused.

Some 5,000 people, a quarter of Victoria's white population at that time, gathered to watch the execution. Some sources say 6,000 were there.[5] The *Port Phillip Herald* recorded:

> An immense crowd . . . between four and five thousand people, the greater part of whom were *women and children*. From the laughing and merry faces which were assembled . . . the scene resembled more the appearance of a race-course than a scene of death. The walls and body of the new gaol were literally packed with spectators as anxiously awaiting the awful scene as if it were a bull-bait or a prize-ring.[6]

Many came with picnic baskets. The publican, Byng, a Republican Negro from the USA, turned up on a prancing white horse. Bushmen, all jovial and excited, came in to celebrate wearing their best gear, buff breeches and top boots, their spurs shining. They poured into town from all the surrounding stations. People even stood on the open coffins lying near the gallows in order to see better. Some Aborigines had climbed up in the trees overlooking the gallows. A detachment of infantry paraded in their Sunday best while they awaited the arrival of the condemned.

Then Jack and Bob arrived in a sombre procession 'escorted by the constabulary and the mounted police', accompanied by civic authorities. The cart drew up near the three-and-a-half-metre-high scaffold. It was a flimsy structure with a platform so narrow that there was scarcely room for the executioner. The trap-door, through which they would fall, was propped up with a pile of bricks and pieces of wood.

They got down from the cart. There was then a twenty minute 'farce of prayer reading', as the *Port Phillip Gazette* described it. The chaplain was frequently interrupted by impatient shouts of 'Cut it short!' The crowd surged about them, giving vent to 'explosions of uproarious merriment'.[7]

Meanwhile, Jack remained calm, but Bob was overcome with terror. 'They knelt together with the clergyman . . . on rising again, Bob's feelings broke out in the most heart-rending groans; the terrified and piteous looks he threw around him . . . was terrible to witness; he trembled violently.'

In the crowd, horrified at all he saw, was one of the Assistant Protectors, James Dredge. He recorded the events in his diary.

This morning, amidst hundreds - perhaps thousands - of spectators . . . such an affecting, appalling, disgusting execrable scene my eyes never saw - God forbid they should ere behold the like again.[8]

The executioner tied their hands before they went up the ladder and chains hung from their ankles, making it nearly impossible for them.

The poor wretches, in getting up the ladder, deprived of the use of their hands, were obliged to cling to the bars with their knees and chins and be partly dragged and partly pushed up to slaughter . . .

Jack was the first to ascend the ladder which he did with tolerable firmness. Poor Bob had to be literally dragged to the fatal platform.[9]

When Jack was on the platform at the top of the ladder, Bob was still saying goodbye to various people in the crowd, reportedly hoping someone might reprieve him, 'pressing against everyone that spoke to him as if to catch at some chance of salvation.' Jack took his place by the noose. He showed no signs of fear and asked the executioner not to cover his eyes so he could see Bob come up beside him.

When Bob eventually staggered to the foot of the ladder he was on the point of collapse. He could not manage to climb it and the executioner had to come down to drag him up.

The crowd hushed as Bob was dragged up into sight. The heckling and merriment vanished as they saw him shaking violently on the platform. Jack also began to shake from seeing his friend so terror-struck. The executioner feared they might panic. The platform was so flimsy that it needed very little for him to lose his own balance and fall into the crowd. He fixed the nooses, pulled down the night-caps and hurried down the ladder. He and his assistant took hold of the rope that would pull away the trapdoor's support.

The preacher stood below reading out prayers in a loud voice. As he said the key words 'In the midst of life we are in death', the trapdoor opened and Jack and Bob fell. But they only fell a short distance, not enough to jerk them and break their necks. They writhed on the ropes as they half dangled, blind-folded and in shock. 'There was a dead pause, and a cry of shame from the crowd.'[10] The two ... twisted and writhed convulsively in a manner that horrified even the most hardened.'[11]

Then the piece of timber holding up the trap was kicked away and they fell to the full length of the rope. Jack was killed instantly, but Bob's noose had been incorrectly placed or had dislodged. He continued to struggle wildly, 'his chest labouring and heaving violently, his fine athletic frame was dreadfully convulsed.'[12] Thus 'the unhappy victims were bunglingly and rudely consigned to their fate.'

By this stage the mood of the crowd had changed to anger. Insults were hurled at the executioner, Davies,* who could only grin sheepishly. The papers reported that 'the circumstances were a gross insult to public decency and should be noted by the proper authorities.'[13]

The bodies hung for the regulation hour and were then taken down. They were probably then stripped of their clothing, for this was a regular perk for executioners. Once in the waiting coffins, the bodies went by cart to the Aboriginal graveyard outside Melbourne's cemetery (now the site of the Victoria Market) where Robinson was awaiting them by open graves.

---

* John Davies was promised a ticket of leave and £10/-/- for executing the Aborigines.[14] But Sydney authorities afterwards would only give him £5/-/- and only after ·much pressure did he get his ticket in November next year, 1843.

Chapter Nine
The Sequel

The Tasmanians

Robinson was highly annoyed when he was charged with personal responsibility for the acquitted women by Judge Willis. He had only been discharged of this responsibility a year and a half earlier at his own request.[1]

However, much to Robinson's relief, La Trobe offered to pay to repatriate not just the women, but all the Van Diemen's Land Aborigines. Six months after the trial, five were returned to Flinders Island. Two, Peter Brune and Johnny Franklin, remained in Victoria. They were all who survived out of the seventeen who came to Port Phillip.*

The rebel women, Truganini, Fanny and Matilda, became noted spokespeople for their race. They introduced new forms of traditional dances, fresh supplies of ochre and strengthened traditional culture.[2] They, with the others who returned from Port Phillip, Davy Bruny, Jack Allen, Mary Anne and Walter Arthur, had a greater understanding of what few rights remained to them.

They refused to work without pay, to the amazement of those who had not left the island since arrival. They sought better living conditions, much to the horror of the white superintendent, Jeanneret.[3] He believed they should *earn* better conditions; the Aborigines thought they had a *right* to decent conditions as a

---

* A party of six actually returned to Flinders Island, but one of them, Jack Allen, was not part of the original party but went to Port Phillip with Batman.

compensation for the loss of their land – a conflict of views that has continued in Australia until today. They told Jeanneret that the Flinders Island settlement had been created for the benefit of the whites, not the Aborigines. There was much validity in their argument given the enormous jump in land values once the Aborigines had been removed to the island. (See official correspondence quoted earlier, page 12.)

The Flinders Island community was further increased at the end of 1842 when the last Aboriginal family known to be still on the mainland was captured by a sealer at Woolnorth.[4] But there were still only about fifty-five to sixty in the community. They protested against having a European superintendent. One of them, Walter Arthur, wrote to a Quaker in Hobart that all they wanted was land so they could be independent. In 1846 the Flinders Island community petitioned Queen Victoria to restore to them some land and asked for the removal of Jeanneret, whom they saw as a despot.[5]

Walter Arthur wrote, 'We black people are threatened by Dr Jeanneret to be hanged if we write anymore about him . . . we are threatened to be put in gaol . . . we are threatened to have our rations stopped if we do not work.'[6]

Mary Anne wrote that 'Dr Jeanneret talks plenty about . . . that he will hang us for writing this letter to the Queen from our countrypeople . . . we do not like to be his slaves.'[7]

Because of their protests, the Colonial Office in London and the Tasmanian authorities decided to close down the Flinders Island settlement and move them back to the mainland of Tasmania.

James Stephen, the Under-Secretary at the Colonial Office, wrote that he could not understand why they should continue a settlement so costly to settlers and 'so fatal' to Aborigines, 'particularly as the establishment had been created not so much with a view to any benefit to [the Aborigines] as from a regard to the interests of the colonialists.'[8]

He also expressed a fear that the offspring of the sealers and Aboriginal women would become a charge on the government if the Aborigines were to stay there.

Truganini was one of those whom he wanted to remove from the sealers. Jeanneret complained strongly about the 'immorality' of Truganini and Matilda, another of the Port Phillip rebels, particularly because they absconded from the official Aboriginal settlement to stay with the sealers in their community. Many Aborigines much preferred the sealers, who had taken Aboriginal wives and had Aboriginal children, to Jeanneret's harsh regime.

Jeanneret even tried to curb Truganini by 'marrying' her to an Aborigine in the settlement; all quite illegal, as he had no authority to perform marriages.[9] (This was a repeat of Robinson's earlier matrimonial strategy.)

Truganini once owned that she was not popular with many of her fellow Tasmanians because they held her responsible for having worked with Robinson to remove them from their tribal lands. She was told that as a punishment it would be her fate to live to be the last of them.

In 1847 Truganini, with forty-five other Aborigines, was removed, in the oddly-named ship *I Don't Know*, from the official Flinders Island settlement to a former penal station at Oyster Cove near Hobart and Jeanneret was dismissed. Forty-seven stayed on in the islands in the sealers' communities.

The white settlers feared the return of even these few Van Diemen's Land Aborigines. A public meeting in Launceston on 30 September 1847 protested against the return of 'these savages to their primitive home', saying it was a waste of good agricultural land to give Oyster Cove to the Aborigines.[10]

Oyster Cove was no paradise. It had previously been abandoned as a convict station because it was too damp and unsanitary to meet even convict standards. Sending the Aborigines there was practically to condemn them to death, given their susceptibility to introduced respiratory diseases. Twenty-nine of them died in the next seven years leaving only seventeen. Then, in 1855, the government expelled those they knew to be of mixed blood. By 1868 only three Aborigines remained alive at Oyster Cove.

As these last few in the official settlement died, there was a ghoulish struggle by scientists for parts of their bodies. The scientists reckoned the Tasmanian Aborigines were even more ancient as a race than the mainland Aborigines and therefore their bodies would be evidence of how humankind had evolved. Their very racist evolutionary theory had Europeans at the head of the evolutionary ladder and Aborigines at its foot.

Evolutionary theories were evolved that justified the extinction of the Aborigines under the 'natural law of survival of the fittest'. The evolutionist H K Rusden, explained in 1876:

> The survival of the fittest means that might is right. And thus we invoke and remorselessly fulfill the inexorable law of natural selection when exterminating the inferior Australian and Maori races – and we appropriate their patrimony coolly.[11]

The last male to die, William Lanney, Truganini's mate, had his skull stolen by Dr Crowther who wished to send it to the Royal College of Surgeons in London. He swapped it for a skull on a white corpse, roughly inserting it inside the skin of Lanney's head. Lanney's hands and feet were then stolen by members of the rival Royal Society of Tasmania. Later, after his funeral, the Members of the Royal Society, beating Dr Crowther to the graveyard by an hour, dug up the coffin, threw back the unwanted white skull, took out Lanney's body and divided it between them.[12] Dr Stokell of the Royal Society made a tobacco pouch from some of Lanney's skin.

Lanney's family had lived in freedom in Tasmania until after the others returned from Port Phillip. He was part of the group who were only captured in December 1842.

The Oyster Cove Aboriginal cemetery was later excavated, yielding for scientists a further eleven skulls. After these horrific activities became public, Truganini begged that she be buried in the deepest part of the D'Entrecasteaux Channel, in her tribal fishing grounds, so her skull would not be taken.[13]

Mary Anne died in 1871, leaving Truganini the only survivor at Oyster Cove. But she was not the last Tasmanian Aborigine. Others had stayed up at Flinders Island and on nearby islands, living in the sealers' communities, carrying on their traditional mutton-birding and sealing. There were rumours, too, of other Aborigines who had never been captured and who still lived free on the Tasmanian mainland.

In 1872 she received an invitation from Lucy Beedon, one of the leaders of those still up in the islands, for her to rejoin them, but Truganini declined. At Oyster Bay she was close to her traditional tribal grounds and could visit the places important to her. At that time there were eighty-four Tasmanian Aborigines on Cape Barren Island alone. As fifty-two of these were children, it promised well for the survival of the race although, to the scientists' regret, no longer a 'pure-blooded' race.

In 1876, at the age of sixty-four, Truganini died. Her wishes were not respected. She was not buried at sea off her tribal lands. In 1878 the Royal Society of Tasmania dug up her body and displayed her skeleton in their museum. There was no respect for her in death, just as there had been no respect for her or her people in life. Her skeleton stood amid a display of tribal artifacts, with a sign underneath saying:

LALLAH ROOKE OR TRUGANINI: THE LAST TASMANIAN ABORIGINE

It was sent across briefly to Melbourne in 1888 and 1904.

It was not until 1976 that the Tasmanian government heeded Aboriginal protests and, overriding the objections of the museum authorities with legislation, had her body cremated. Next day, 1 May 1876, her ashes were scattered on her tribal fishing grounds in the D'Entrecasteaux Channel by members of the surviving Tasmanian Aboriginal community.[14]

Only Truganini's skull could be positively identified as hers among the bones cremated. It had been separated from the rest of the skeleton. There was doubt about the rest of the skeleton being Truganini's for it was several inches taller than Truganini's reputed height.[15]

Unknown to scientists, two 'full-blooded' Tasmanian women survived Truganini up in the islands. Betty and Suke from Cape Portland lived on Kangaroo Island until 1878 and 1888 respectively. There are reports that two male Aborigines were shot at Port Davey some years after Truganini's death. There are accounts today among descendants of the survivors that others escaped detection on the mainland.

Those remaining on the Bass Strait islands struggled constantly to have their Aboriginality officially recognized. But from 1850 the state government refused to do this, despite seven full-blood women being in the community. The government wanted no other charge on the public purse than the one official Aboriginal settlement at Oyster Cove.

In the twentieth century, more and more Aborigines left the islands to live on the mainland, although strong island communities still survive. It was not until 1971 that these descendants of the first Tasmanians were to receive government recognition as Aborigines rather than as 'islanders'.

The Victorians

The executions did not bring a respite for the Port Phillip settlers – nor for the Aborigines. While the Van Diemen's Land men were still in custody before the execution, the *Port Phillip Herald* reported several complaints by people living around the Plenty River.

'The desperadoes are well supplied with fire-arms with the use of which they seem as well acquainted as the whites.'[16]

The same issue of the *Port Phillip Advertiser* that carried the news of their death sentence, reported:

GIPPS LAND: The blacks, we understand, have assembled in great numbers in Gipps Land and openly menace the lives of the settlers who are perfectly unprotected. A party of no less than 600 recently attacked a station belonging to Mr Macalister but were fortunately repulsed.[17]

Meyrick, in his letters, reported horrific massacres of the blacks around the Macalister River.[18] There may have been some connection. No Protector was stationed out there to investigate these reports.

On 20 September 1842, the Port Phillip Debating Society conducted a three-day debate before a packed audience.[19] Only men were allowed to speak, although the *Port Phillip Gazette* regretted the exclusion of women. The question for debate was: *Is Uncivilized Man Benefited By His Intercourse With Civilized Man?* The result: the following motion was carried with 'only one left hand raised to the contrary': *Uncivilized Man Has Not Benefited*.

From 1835-49, William Thomas's records show that fifty-seven Aborigines were arrested in Victoria. Of the thirty-three who came to trial, five were hanged, thirteen transported (removed to Tasmania or elsewhere) and six imprisoned. Nine were found not guilty. No European in Port Phillip was convicted of killing an Aborigine until 1848 and then he was only given two months imprisonment.

There were four public hangings in Melbourne in 1842. Three were bushrangers, Ellis, Jepps and Fogarty, who operated around Dandenong and the Plenty River. They were hanged in June on a brand-new, re-erectable gallows costing four times as much as the one used to hang the Tasmanians.[20] The authorities were not risking a repeat of the events at the Aborigines' execution. The last public hanging was another Aborigine known as Roger the Russian.

Roger was accused of killing a white man, Patrick Codd, in May 1840. The settlers had taken immediate revenge at that time, killing the first five Aborigines they could find. They were not brought before the courts. Roger maintained that he was innocent right to the end.

Codd's death, according to Robinson, was related to his killing of Aborigines on the Wedge Station on the Grange River where the local Aborigines had strongly resisted their land being taken. The Aborigines constantly harassed the station, driving off some 1,300 sheep worth about £2,000. Wedge mounted a swivel-gun on his station and used it on Aborigines. Codd assisted him.[21] Codd was killed working on John Cox's station near Mt Rouse, an area densely populated by Aborigines. Cox had admitted shooting down several Aborigines 'without hesitation or regret' for stealing sheep.

In February 1842 La Trobe made inquiries into a reported killing of Aborigines by settlers by Muston Creek, also near Mt Rouse. On July 15 he reported:

A party of aboriginal natives consisting of two males, four females and two children were surprised while resting in a tea-tree shrub not far from Smith and Osbrey's station by a party of White men, probably eight in number who, after dismounting, killed by pistol or gun-shot wounds three of the women and a child on the spot, and grievously wounding another female – since dead . . . It is further satisfactorily shown that the natives attacked neither were a marauding party nor in any way connected with one of that character.[22]

Six whites were brought before a magistrate; three of them were committed to trial. But when they came up before Judge Willis, he berated the government for spending time bringing the killers of lubras to court when the murderers of whites went free. He acquitted all three whites.

Roger was arrested in March 1842 when he was identified by Codd's brother, Clement. Aboriginal witnesses stated that he was not on Cox's station at the time of the killing, but their evidence was unacceptable to the court. Roger said he was assisting with sheep-washing on another station at the time. He named the whites he was working with but his alibi was never checked. Willis sentenced him and he was publicly hanged on 5 September 1842.[23]

La Trobe admitted he doubted Roger's guilt. He said he knew Codd's behaviour had been 'criminal in the highest possible degree' towards the natives.[24] Roger himself said that although he had not killed Codd, Codd deserved to die for abusing black women. Lord Stanley wrote later from London to Governor Gipps, reproving him for not considering La Trobe's views.[25]

This was the last execution for many years – until 1847. In 1854 public executions were forbidden in Victoria on the grounds that they were demoralizing. All executions in future were to be within gaols.[26]

Out in the bush things went on much as before. Henry Meyrick wrote from his run on the Mornington Peninsula to his father, the Reverend Meyrick of Avebury in Wiltshire.

> The blacks are fast disappearing from the face of the earth. Of our tribe there are but eight men and children and one woman left. Rum is killing those who we civilize and the white men are shooting those we do not. The Protectorate System is the most grievous humbug. It is a tremendous expense, and there's never by any accident a single black on the Protectorate Station. The wise Protectors are in the habit of burying the dead on the stations which, alone, would keep away the Blacks forever.[27]

In the Western District, guerrilla warfare reached its highest point in the year of Bob's and Jack's deaths, 1842. That year Aborigines drove off about 4,000 sheep, using some to stock their own secret stations with yards concealed in the Grampians and elsewhere.[28] Four whites were killed in these attacks. The Aborigines concentrated on stations established on traditional Aboriginal meeting grounds and sacred places near Port Fairy, Lake Condah, Mt Rouse and Mt Napier.[29]

Port Fairy settlers appealed to La Trobe for assistance saying 'some of our number intend leaving the district wholly and entirely on account of the natives. Their numbers, their ferocity and their cunning, render them peculiarly formidable.'[30] The *Portland Mercury* reported in August 1842 that 'The region may just as well be in a state of war.'

In Gippsland, according to the *Jubilee History of Victoria*, there was a 'general hunt after the blacks' in 1842 in the Bruthen Creek area where 'a camp was surrounded [and] they were shot by hundreds.' Despite this, Aboriginal attacks on Gippsland stations continued into the 1850s.

The role of Aboriginal trackers in catching the Tasmanians gave impetus to the idea of setting up a Native Police Corps. Twenty Aboriginal men were recruited the month after Bob's and Jack's execution; Henry Dana, a Western District squatter, was put in charge of them.[31] They were given a dashing uniform – green jacket with possum trimmings, red stripes up the trousers – but no pay. Only Dana was to be paid regularly. The Aborigines received food rations as their pay. This highly economical force was based at Dandenong and operated almost exclusively against Aborigines for the ten years it existed.

It was highly efficient, too, much to the delight of the squatters. On one occasion, in August 1843, they killed twenty Aborigines for stealing 180 sheep from Purbrick's Koroite station on the Wannon River. The *Port Phillip Gazette* reported that the squatters were 'in perfect ecstasies', declaring a 'real service has been done for them.'[32]

When Protector Thomas asked one of the Aboriginal troopers why they killed Aborigines who stole rather than take them into custody as happened with whites who stole, he answered: 'Captain said "You blackfellows no shoot them, me handcuff you and send you to jail." ' They did catch a few; these they flogged until 'the blood spurted over the bystanders.'[33]

In August 1843 there were massive attacks by parties of up to 600 Aborigines on stations along the Murray, forcing several settlers out of the district. These attacks continued throughout 1844 and 1845. On 16 December 1845, the *Port Phillip Patriot* reported soldiers sent to the Murray because of trouble with blacks. The Aborigines used the flooded river plains as a refuge making it impossible for the troopers to catch them. After this there were strong rumours of Aborigines being poisoned en masse along the Murray. Police reports identified 'damper laced with corrosive sublimate' as in use down near Mt Gambier.[34]

But the flood of white immigrants continued unabated. The recession in the early 1840s ended, but not before many had to sell up their flocks and herds to pay the bills they could not meet without a crop or clip. Of the 481 who held pastoral leases around Port Phillip in 1840, half had left by 1845. But the newcomers in 1844-5 lifted the number of leases taken to 850.

Meyrick had survived because he did not go into town on drunken orgies as did many of his contemporaries under pressure of life in the bush. He remained as self-sufficient as he could and as clear of debt as possible. He was scornful of those who were not prudent.

> The joyous days of old are fast returning. The squatters are beginning again to buy tandems and to spend their money in the same wise manner they did before. I saw a fellow buying gig and harness for a great deal more than it was worth. When he was told that the gig would be no use to him, as it was so lightly built that it would fall into pieces in the bush, he made answer "It is very true, but what can a man do with his money?" This wretched idiot had but 1,000 sheep of his own.[35]

It was not long before Meyrick, worn down and exhausted, decided to move from WesternPort to the Gippsland mountains. In a rushed and tired hand he wrote on 3 February 1846, 'No man can thrive in this accursed Western Port. We have worked hard and lived on salt beef and damper for nearly six years to no purpose.'[36]

On 5 February he started off on a month-long trek into the Gippsland bush, he had found an unoccupied site on the Macalister River where it runs in a long, deep valley from the Australian Alps to the coastal plains. Maurice, his cousin, was taking an adjacent run. 'Our huts will only be a few hundred yards apart on the river.'[37]

On 11 April he described his run. 'It would not suit anyone who could not make himself happy anywhere, inasmuch as it is very much like a large gaol – twenty-five miles from the nearest settler and surrounded for eight months of the year with snow.' The river was a 'mountain torrent and the only road I am yet to find crosses the river eleven times', cutting him off much of the year.[38]

His life was incredibly hard. His talk of building a hut proved over-optimistic. He wrote to his mother on 30 October 1846 from a 'neighbouring' station.

I write lest you should should think I am speared by the blacks. I am living under a tarpaulin and have been doing so for nearly twelve months. I have no fixed place of abode. I have no candle, table, pen, ink or paper, so that it's only when I get away for the day that I can write. I like the run very much.[39]

He went on to say what he had learnt of the treatment of the Gippsland Aborigines since he arrived there.

The blacks are very quiet here now, poor wretches. No wild beast of the forest was ever hunted down with such unsparing perseverance as they are; men, women and children are shot down when ever they can be met with . . . Some excuse might be found for shooting the men by those who are getting their cattle speared, but what . . . is their excuse who shoot the women and children, I cannot conceive.

I have protested against it at every station I have been in to Gibbs in the strongest language, but these things are kept very secret as the penalty would certainly be hanging. Maurice was out with a party after the blacks but refused to fire on them (as did another of the party) to the intense indignation of the rest of the party who returned leaving them unmolested.

For myself, if I caught a black actually killing my sheep, I would shoot him with as little remorse as I would a wild dog, but no consideration on earth would induce me to ride into a camp and fire on them indiscriminately as is the custom here whenever their smoke is seen.

I have become so familiarized with scenes of horror – from hearing murder made a topic of everyday conversation. I have heard tales told and some things I have seen that would form as dark a page as ever you read in the book of history, but I thank God that I have never participated in them.

If I could remedy these things I would speak loudly thou' it cost me all I am worth in the world, but as I cannot, I will keep aloof and know nothing and say nothing.[40]

Meyrick lived on there for about another year. Life did not get any easier for him. A year later he still had no hut. Having become ill with rheumatism from the constant exposure and the damp, he sold the run. On 17 October 1847 he wrote his last letter home, a resume of his life in Australia and all his trials. He said he felt a richer and wiser man for his experiences and added: 'It is a current saying that a man who has lived here can match the devil himself. It certainly is the most lawless place I ever heard of.'[41]

These were the last words he wrote home. Shortly afterwards he drowned in the Thompson River while swimming across to seek help for a pregnant woman.[42]

*

Aboriginal armed resistance did not end in Victoria until the 1850s. By then over thirteen years of guerrilla warfare and settler attacks had exhausted and decimated the tribes. The gold-rush was the final straw. It swamped the tribes. In 1851 there were 77,000 whites in Victoria; by 1861 there were 540,000!

At the time Melbourne was founded the original Aboriginal population had already been decimated by plagues. It had dropped from perhaps 100,000[43] to about 15,000-20,000. In 1861 the Central Board for the Protection of Aborigines estimated Aboriginal numbers at only 2341.

Despite the recommendations of Judge Willis, there was never any real attempt to establish any substantial reserves for the Port Phillip [Victorian] Aborigines. Only a scattering of small reserves and missions were ever set aside.

A school for Aborigines was established near the junction of Merri Creek and the Yarra River, provoking the strongest opposition. The *Geelong Advertiser* said:

All measures taken to the eventual civilisation of future generations are founded on an illusion. The perpetuation of the Aboriginal race is not to be desired – it is no more desirable that any inferior race should be perpetuated than that the transmission of an hereditary disease such as scrofula or insanity should be encouraged.[44]

In 1863, sixty Aborigines of the Kulin Confederation, including the Wurundjeri tribe of the Yarra and the Taungurong of the Goulburn, picked out land near the present site of Healesville to be the home of their people. Through their spokesmen, Barak and Wonga of the Wurundjeri, they approached the state government for this land. As the Aborigines were no longer seen as a threat, the government granted their wishes. They called their reserve, Corranderrk, after a local, white-flowering tea-tree.[45]

However, the continuing strength of the surviving Aboriginal communities concerned the government. The self-supporting Corranderrk community constantly campaigned for full Aboriginal control over Aboriginal affairs. So did other communities at Framlingham, Lake Condah, up on the Murray and elsewhere.

The government took steps to counter this. In 1886 a law was passed barring all 'half-caste' Aborigines from the reserves.[46] This tore children from their mothers, breaking up many families, seriously weakening communities. This law was designed to limit the number of those called 'Aborigines', to lessen their charge on the government. It was the identical motive to that of the Tasmanian government when it refused to recognize the 'Aboriginality' of those who stayed on the islands and did not go to Oyster Cove. It was presumed that once the last of the full-bloods died, the Victorian Aborigines, like the Tasmanians, would be extinct.*

However, the state government still did not have control over the 'full-bloods' and over their potential land claims. Most continued to live outside the church missions and government reserves. A census in 1869 found that only one quarter of the surviving Aborigines were on Aboriginal stations. This disturbed the government; they looked with favour on Tasmania's solution of removing them all to one remote location. The first step to achieving this was the

---

* One could imagine the upset if the British government defined the Welsh, or even the English, in such a way!

passage of a law in 1869 under which Aborigines could be told where they were to live.[47]

Barak and nine other Aborigines wrote to the newspapers in protest. 'It seems that we are going to be treated like slaves. Are we prisoners or convicts? We should think we are all free as any white man of the colony.'[48]

Under this law, the Corranderrk Reserve was eventually closed and members of the Yarra and Goulburn tribes transferred to a distant part of Gippsland, Lake Tyers. Other small reserves around Victoria were also closed – in the interests of 'economy' –and the Aborigines transferred to Lake Tyers. Soon it was the only official Aboriginal settlement in Victoria, the Victorian equivalent of Flinders Island.

In 1965 the government moved to disperse the Aborigines remaining there, but failed. Lake Tyers is still an Aboriginal settlement. Recently, the Aborigines living there were given some security of tenure. A few Aboriginal people of the Western District have also secured some land for their communities at the former missions of Lake Condah and of Framlingham near Warrnambool. Similar moves in Tasmania have given the local Aborigines rights to one small, uninhabited Bass Strait island.

In 1985, Victoria's 150th Anniversary year, the Aborigines who died for their country still lie uncommemorated. Their struggle is forgotten. Yet, in the centre of every small Victorian town, a cenotaph honours the dead of distant wars.

Little wonder then that the current efforts by Victorian Aboriginal communities to recover a small part of their lost land are also receiving scant public recognition or support. This state still has no Aboriginal land-rights law, no appropriate compensation measures. Victorian 'patriotism' is blinkered indeed.

It is obvious that the struggle of Jack, Bob, Matilda, Fanny, Truganini and their compatriots is far from over.

Endnotes

Chapter 1

1. Henry Meyrick, *Letter* to his mother, 1 November 1840, manuscript copy held at La Trobe Library, Melbourne.
2. *Port Phillip Herald*, 29 October 1841.
3. Truganini is pronounced Truc-a-nee-ni.
4. For the information in this chapter the author is particularly endebted to Lyndall Ryan, *The Aboriginal Tasmanians*, University of Queensland Press, St Lucia, Queensland, 1981, and to Vivienne Rae Ellis, *Trucanini*, Australian Institute of Aboriginal Studies, Canberra, 1981.
5. N J B Plomley, *Friendly Mission: The Tasmanian Journals and Papers of G A Robinson, 1829-34*, Tasmanian Historical Research Association, 1966.
6. Plomley, quoted in Ryan, pp.135-7; also A L Meston, *The Van Diemen's Land Company*, Records of the Queen Victoria Museum, Launceston, pp.825-4.
7. ibid.
8. ibid.
9. Plomley, p.180, quoted in Ryan, pp.137-8.
10. op. cit., p.394, quoted in Ryan, p.154.
11. Ryan, p.151.
12. Colonial Secretary to Robinson, 10 February, 1832.
13. British Parliament, *Papers*, 1831, no.259, vol.19, p.55, quoted in Ryan, p.97.
14. Robinson, *Flinders Island Journal*, 17 October 1837.
15. Ryan, p.141.
16. J E Calder, *Some Account of the Wars, Extirpation, Habits, etc. of the Native Tribes of Tasmania*, 1875, Hobart, p.104, quoted in Ellis, p.9.
17. Calder, pp.104-6, quoted in Ellis, p.25.
18. Van Diemen's Land Executive Council, *Minutes*, 31 October 1828.
19. Plomley, *Private Correspondence* with Ellis, 12 January 1976, quoted in Ellis, p.38.
20. Plomley, p.647, quoted in Ellis, p.68.
21. Robinson to Colonial Secretary, 3 February 1835.
22. Robinson, *Personal Journal*, 8 February 1836.
23. Robinson, *Flinders Island Journal*, 10 October 1837.

Chapter 2

1. Robinson to John Montagu, 11 February 1835, Select Committee, House of Commons, 1837. This and subsequently quoted documents from the Public Records Office, London, can also be found in *Historical Records of Victoria*, Chapter 1, vol.2A, 1982, Victorian Government Printing Office.
2. ibid.

3. ibid.
4. Sir George Arthur to Lord Glenelg, 21 October 1835, Public Records Office, London, Colonial Office, 280/60.
5. Lord Glenelg to Sir George Arthur, 13 April 1836, Public Records Office, London, Colonial Office, 280/12.
6. Gordon Gairdner to Sir George Grey, 9 July 1837, Public Records Office, London, Colonial Office, 280/69.
7. Sir George Arthur to Lord Glenelg, 22 July 1837, Public Records Office, London, Colonial Office, 280/84.
8. ibid.
9. John Montagu for Sir John Franklin to the Colonial Secretary, 22 August 1838; Sir John Franklin to Lord Glenelg, 13 February 1839, Public Records Office, London Colonial Office, 280/105.
10. John Montagu, op. cit.
11. Report from NSW Legislative Council Committee appointed to inquire into present state of the Aborigines, 12 October 1838, Public Records Office, London, Colonial Office 201/277. For this and subsequently quoted London Colonial Office documents, also see *Historical Records of Victoria*, Chapter 15, Vol.2B, 1983, Victorian Government Printing Office.
12. Sir George Gipps to Lord Glenelg, 10 November 1838, Public Records Office, London, Colonial Office, 280/105.
13. ibid., *Minute* attached by James Stephen, 9 May 1839.
14. ibid.
15. *NSW Government Gazette*, 12 December 1838.
16. Robinson to La Trobe, 8 November, 12 December 1839, Public Records Office, Victoria.
17. Chief Protector's Office, *Receipt*, 31 December 1839, Public Records Office, Victoria.
18. Colonial Secretary to La Trobe, 17 December 1859, Public Records Office, Victoria.
19. Robinson to La Trobe, 12 December 1839, Public Records Office, Victoria.
20. *Launceston Chronicle*, 10 May 1836.
21. Noel Butler, *Our Original Aggression*.
22. Watkin Tench, *Sydney's First Four Years*, c.April 1789, being a reprint of *A Narrative of the Expedition to Botany Bay*, first published London, 1789, and *A Complete Account of the Settlement at Port Jackson*, first published London 1793, Angus and Robertson 1961, quoted in Keith Willey, *When the Sky Fell Down*, Collins, 1979, p.72.
23. William Bradley, *A Voyage to New South Wales. The Journal of Lieutenant William Bradley, RN, of* HMS Sirius *1786-92*, Ure Smith, Sydney, 1969, quoted in Willey, pp.72-3.
24. Richard Broome, *Arriving*, vol.1 in *The Victorians*, 1985.
25. George Langhorne, in *Miscellaneous Papers* collected by Harry F Gurner, Mitchell Library, Sydney.
26. ibid.
27. ibid.
28. ibid; also J F Meyrick, *Life in the Bush, 1840-7*, Nelson, 1939.
29. J H Wedge, 15 March 1836, in vol.1 of *Historical Records of Victoria*, pp.34-5.

110 Jack of Cape Grim: A Victorian Adventure

30. Sir Richard Burke, *Proclamation*, 3 May 1836, reproduced in vol.2a, *Historical Records of Victoria*, p.38.
31. John Montagu, for Governor Arthur, to Colonial Secretary, 18 August 1836.
32. Garryowen, *Chronicles of Early Melbourne, 1835-52*, Ferguson and Mitchell, Melbourne 1858, p.203.
33. ibid., p.184.
34. W P Faithful to Colonial Secretary, 8 May 1838, NSW Archives.
35. Dr George E Mackay, from Lewis's Station, Hume River, to W Broughton of Burrowa, River Murray, 15 May 1838, sent on to Colonial Secretary; also Police Magistrate George Stewart to Colonial Secretary, *Report*, 20 June 1838.
36. *Australian*, 8 December 1838, in M F Christie, *Aborigines in Colonial Victoria 1835-86*, Sydney University Press, 1979. p.45. This book is highly recommended for further study.
37. William Thomas, *Journal*, 1 April 1839, Mitchell Library, Sydney.
38. Phillip King, et al. to Sir George Gipps, 8 June 1838, Royal Historical Society of Victoria.
39. Colonial Secretary to Phillip King and other memorialists, 23 June 1838, Return to Address, House of Commons, 12 August 1839.

Chapter 3

1. H H Meyrick, *Letters* to his family, 1840-47, La Trobe Library, Manuscript 7957.
2. Niel Black, *Diary*, copy held at La Trobe Library, Manuscript 8996.
3. Charles Buchett, *The Gums*, 1839.
4. Black, *Diary*, 12 December 1840.
5. Moonin Moonin, quoted by James Dredge in his *Diary*, entry for 6 December 1839, typescript copy, La Trobe Library, Melbourne. Also quoted in Christie, p.41.
6. Katherine Kirkland, in Richard Broome.
7. Sievwright to Earl Grey, 8 March 1847, in Christie, p.44.
8. H H Meyrick, *Life in the Bush, 1840-47*, Nelson, 1939.
9. F J Meyrick, Nelson, 1939, pp.104ff.
10. Buckley, quoted by George Langhorne in *Miscellaneous Papers* collected by Harry Gurner, Mitchell Library, Sydney.
11. *Port Phillip Gazette*, 6 July 1842.
12. *Port Phillip Herald*, 12 November 1841.
13. *Chronicles of Early Melbourne*, p.188.

Chapter 4

1. William Thomas, *Journal*, 17-18 January 1839, Mitchell Library, Sydney.
2. Thomas, op. cit., 12 February 1839.
3. ibid., 5 February 1839.
4. Robinson to La Trobe, 23 December 1839.

Endnotes 111

5. ibid., April 1839.
6. Reverend J R Orton, *Journal*, 19 April 1839, La Trobe Library.
7. Thomas, Report, 1 December to 1 March 1844, Box 12, APR, PRO, Victoria (hereinafter cited as PROVic).
8. ibid.
9. Thomas, *Journal*, April 1839.
10. ibid., 5 May 1839.
11. ibid., 6 May 1839.
12. Dr P E Cussen to Robinson, 6 May 1839.
13. Robinson to Colonial Secretary, 13 May 1839; Colonial Secretary's *Minute* with document, n.d.
14. Governor's *Minute* with above, 3 June 1839.
15. Thomas, *Journal*, 2 June 1839.
16. Robinson to La Trobe, 17 August 1840.
17. Thomas, *Journal*, 20 August 1839.
18. Thomas, *Journal*, 21-25 August 1839.
19. Robinson to Thomas, 2 September 1839, NSW Archives.
20. Thomas, *Journal*, 8 September 1839.
21. Robinson to Assistant Protectors, 8 July 1839.
22. Robinson to La Trobe, 17 August 1840.
23. Snodgrass, *Letter* enclosed with La Trobe to Gipps, 4 April 1840, Colonial Secretary, Inward Mail, 4/2510, Archives Office, NSW.
24. Thomas to Robinson, 12 March 1841.
25. Thomas, *Memorial to the Governor*, 22 June 1841, with Robinson's Inward Correspondence, PROVic.
26. Thomas, *Report*, 1 June-31 August 1846, Box 12 APR, PROVic.
27. Sievwright to Robinson, 16 March 1839, NSW Archives.
28. Robinson to Colonial Secretary, 13 August 1839, NSW Archives.
29. La Trobe to Robinson, 31 December 1839, PROVic.
30. Dredge to Robinson, 23 July 1839.
31. Dredge, *Journal*, 8 December 1839, La Trobe Library.
32. Parker to Robinson, 1 April 1840, NSW Archives.
33. Robinson to Colonial Secretary, 22 April 1839, NSW Archives; also J H Plunket, Attorney-General, to Colonial Secretary, 25 May 1839, NSW Archives.
34. Sievwright to Robinson, 1 November 1839; also Reverend Benjamin Hurst to Sievwright, 11 November 1839, NSW Archives.
35. Sievwright to Robinson, 22 January 1840, NSW Archives.
36. ibid.

Chapter 5

1. Robinson to Assistant Protectors, 8 July 1839, NSW Archives.
2. Sievwright to Robinson, 17 July 1839, NSW Archives.
3. Thomas, *Journal*, 9 September 1839.
4. ibid., 10 September 1839.
5. ibid., 17 September 1839.
6. ibid., 18 September 1839, note attached.
7. ibid.
8. ibid., 6 & 7 October; see also 21 September 1839.

112 Jack of Cape Grim: A Victorian Adventure

9. ibid., 7 October 1839.
10. Thomas to Robinson, 29 February 1840.
11. Thomas to William Lonsdale, 27 November 1839, PROVic.
12. D G McArthur to Robinson, 17 October 1839, NSW Archives.
13. La Trobe to Robinson, 28 October 1839, NSW Archives.
14. ibid., including Governor's attached *Minute*, 5 December 1839.
15. Robinson to La Trobe, 28 October 1839, NSW Archives.
16. ibid.
17. La Trobe to Robinson, 18 December 1839, PROVic.
18. Thomas to Robinson, 29 February 1840, *Report* on Western Port Aborignes, Remarks, NSW Archives.
19. Thomas to Robinson, 3 January 1840, NSW Archives.
20. Thomas to Robinson, 29 February 1840, *Report*, NSW Archives.
21. H F Gisborne to La Trobe, 15 January 1840.
22. Armyne Bolden to La Trobe, 2 May 1840, PROVic.
23. Docker to Gibbs, 31 December 1840; Robinson to La Trobe, 27 February 1841; Stanley to Gipps, 5 October 1841; see Christie, notes, p.110.
24. Colonial Secretary to Samuel Lettsom, 28 August 1840, with *Despatch 35*, Gipps to Russell, Mitchell Library.
25. La Trobe to Robinson and to Police Magistrates at Melbourne and Geelong, *Circular*, 28 September 1840.
26. Reverend J Orton, *Journal*, A1715, Mitchell Library, p.116.
27. Thomas to Robinson, *Report*, September 1840-February 1841, Box 11, APR, PROVic.
28. La Trobe to Gipps, 4 July 1846, State Library of Victoria.
29. Gipps to La Trobe, 24 October 1840, State Library of Victoria.
30. Thomas, *Journal*, October-December 1840, Mitchell Library, uncatalogued manuscripts, set 214, item 1.
31. Robinson, *Journal*, 4 August 1840, Mitchell Library.
32. Thomas, *Report* for May 1840, series 11, unit 7, doc.308, PROVic.
33. Thomas, *Note*, n.d., series 11, unit 7, doc.291, PROVic.
34. Thomas, *Reminiscences*, uncat. mss., set 214, item 27, Mitchell Library, pp.77-79.

Chapter 6

1. R Massie to La Trobe, 7 October 1841, VPRS 19, Box 20, File 41/1568, PROVic.
2. Samuel Evans, *Deposition*, 30 November 1841, VPRS 24, Box 1, Whalers' Case, (no.43) 1841, PROVic.
3. Massie, op. cit.
4. ibid.
5. *Port Phillip Herald*, 26 November; also Editorial, 24 December 1841.
6. Corporal William Johnson, *Deposition*, 30 November 1841.
7. *Port Phillip Herald*, 24 December 1841.
8. Jamieson to La Trobe, 4 October 1841.
9. *Port Phillip Herald*, 26th November 1891.

10. Samuel Rawson's journal is the main source for much of the rest of this chapter. It is entitled *Journal of An Expedition After Some Van Diemen's Land Blacks Who Were Committing Depredations at Western Port on the Southern Coast of New Holland*, October-November 1841, National Library of Australia, MS 204/1. Powlett's journal was not located, but his official statements to the court were utilized.
11. Rawson, *Journal*, op. cit., p.3.
12. ibid., p.7.
13. La Trobe to Robinson, 31 October 1841, VPRS 16, vol.2, p.342, PROVic.
14. Rawson, *Journal*, op. cit., p.12.
15. ibid., pp.19-21.
16. ibid., p.24.
17. *Port Phillip Herald*, 9 November 1841.
18. Thomas to Robinson, 5 November 1841, VPRS 11, Box 8, item 411, PROVic.
19. Thomas to Robinson, 11 November 1841, VPRS 11, Box 8, item 412, PROVic.
20. Powlett to La Trobe, 16 November 1841, VPRS, Box 22, file 41/1835, PROVic.
21. *Port Phillip Herald*, 26 November 1841.
22. Rawson, *Journal*, op. cit. p.33.
23. ibid., p.34.
24. *Port Phillip Herald*, 29 November 1841.
25. Rawson, *Journal*, pp.39-40.
26. *Port Phillip Herald*, 26 November 1841.
27. Corporal William Johnson, *Deposition*, 30 November 1841.
28. Rawson, *Journal*, op. cit., p.41.

Chapter 7

1. Ian McFarlane, *1842. Public Executions at Melbourne*, Public Records Office, Victoria, 1984. p.2.
2. idem., p.3; also, *Mr Justice J W Willis*, H E Behan, 1979, privately published.
3. U K House of Commons, *Sessional Papers*, 1844, vol.34, *Aborigines*, p.148, Willis's address in Bonjon case.
4. ibid.
5. ibid., pp.144-155.
6. ibid.; also VPRS 16, vol.12, p.296, PROVic, in *Public Executions in Melbourne*, op. cit., p.19.
7. ibid.
8. Russell to Gipps, 11 August 1840, in *Historical Records of Australia*, series 1, vol.20, p.756.
9. *Sydney Morning Herald*, 21 June 1844.
10. *Sydney Morning Herald*, 29 June 1849.
11. *Criminal Record Book*, Prothonotary, 1841-3, December 1841, Melbourne Supreme Court, PROVic.

114 Jack of Cape Grim: A Victorian Adventure

12. House of Commons, *Parliamentary Papers*, vol.34, 1844, Barry's trial notes.
13. ibid.
14. Robert Robins, *Deposition*, House of Commons, *Papers*, op. cit.
15. Watson, *Deposition*, Supreme Court trial, House of Commons, op. cit.
16. ibid., summarized in *Port Phillip Herald*, 21 December 1841.
17. *Port Phillip Herald*, 24 December 1841.
18. *Port Phillip Herald*, 21 January 1842.
19. *Port Phillip Advertiser*, c.24 December 1841.
20. ibid.
21. ibid., separate report on sentencing.
22. Willis to La Trobe, 23 December 1841, VPRS 19, Box 22, file 41/1835.
23. *Port Phillip Herald*, 24 December 1841.
24. *Port Phillip Gazette*, 22 December 1841.
25. ibid.
26. Quoted in MacFarlane, *1842, Public Executions at Melbourne*, p.17.

Chapter 8

1. Robinson, *Journal*, 22 January 1842.
2. *Port Phillip Patriot* and *Melbourne Advertiser*, 24 January 1842.
3. MacFarlane, op. cit., p.59/
4. Robinson, *Journal*, 17 January 1842.
5. H E Behan, *Mr Justice J W Willis*, privately published, 1979.
6. *Port Phillip Herald*, 21 January 1842.
7. Garryowen, *The Chronicles of Early Melbourne: 1835-52*, Melbourne, 1858.
8. Assistant Protector Dredge, *Diary*, 20 January 1842.
9. Garryowen, op. cit.
10. *Port Phillip Gazette*, 22 January 1842.
11. Garryowen, op. cit.
12. Dredge, op. cit.
13. *Port Phillip Gazette*, op.cit.
14. MacFarlane, op. cit., pp.59-60.

Chapter 9

1. Robinson, *Journal*, 25 August 1840.
2. H Jeanneret, *Report on Flinders Island Establishment*, 15 September 1842, State Archives of Tasmania.
3. Lyndall Ryan, *The Aboriginal Tasmanians*, University of Queensland Press, 1981, pp.199-201
4. Jeanneret, *Report*, 31 March 1843.
5. W G Arthur to Walker, 31 December 1845, Mitchell Library, A612, enclosed in Wilmot to Gladstone, 13 August 1846, PRO, London.
6. John Allen Washington, Walter George Arthur and Davy Bruny to Governor, 16 June 1846. PRO, London, Colonial Office 280/195, pp.319-28.
7. Mary Anne Arthur to Governor, 10 June 1846, with above.
8. James Stephen, 30 January 1847. Remarks on *Despatch* of Wilmot to Gladstone, 13 August 1846, PRO, London, CO, 280/27/658.

Endnotes 115

9. Jeanneret, *Report* to Colonial Secretary, 31 March 1843, State Archives of Tasmania.
10. *Launceston Examiner*, 20 October 1847.
11. Jan Roberts, *Massacres to Mining*, Dove, Melbourne, 1981, p.12.
12. *Hobart Mercury*, 9 & 13 March 1869.
13. Dandridge to Colonial Secretary, 8 May 1876, Tasmanian State Archives, CSD 10/31/488; *Hobart Mercury*, 9 May 1876.
14. *Hobart Mercury*, 3 May 1976.
15. Vivienne Ellis, *Trucanini*, Australian Institute of Aboriginal Studies, 1981, pp.171-2.
16. *Port Phillip Herald*, 3 December 1841.
17. *Port Phillip Advertiser*, 22 December 1841.
18. Meyrick, *Letter* to mother, 30 April 1846.
19. *Port Phillip Gazette*, September 1842.
20. MacFarlane, *1842: Public Executions at Melbourne*, p.33.
21. Charles Wedge to John H Wedge, 13 November 1839, in Russell to Gipps, 1 September 1840, Colonial Office, 201.304-5; also Croke to Sievwright, 21 October 1840, *Detached Papers*, Crown Law Office, PROVic.
22. La Trobe, 15 July 1842.
23. *Port Phillip Herald*, 8 September 1842; MacFarlane, op. cit. pp.51-55.
24. MacFarlane, op. cit., fn., p.54.
25. MacFarlane, op. cit., p.56; *Private Letter* from Lord Stanley to Governor Gipps, 6 April 1843.
26. *Act to Regulate the Execution of Criminals*, gazetted 28 November 1854.
27. Meyrick, 18 August 1845.
28. Robinson to La Trobe, 9 April 1842, *Sessional Papers*, House of Commons, 1844, vol.34.
29. M Christie, *Aborigines In Colonial Victoria, 1835-86*, p.62.
30. *Port Phillip Gazette*, 30 March 1842.
31. Christie, op. cit. p.74.
32. *Port Phillip Gazette*, 26 August 1843.
33. Thomas, *Report*, 1 September-1 December 1843; Box 12, APR, PROVic.
34. J C Bryne, *Twelve Years Wanderings In the British Colonies from 1835-1847*, London, 1848, vol.1, p.275; Watton to Robinson, 10 December 1842; Parker to Robinson, 19 February 1849, Box 7, APR, PROVic.
35. Meyrick, 27 September 1845.
36. Meyrick, 3 February 1846.
37. Meyrick, 5 February 1846.
38. Meyrick, 20 February 1846.
39. Meyrick, 30 October 1846.
40. Meyrick, 30 April 1846.
41. Meyrick, 17 October 1847.
42. Richard Broome, *Arriving*, 1985.
43. Noel Butler, *Our Original Aggression*.
44. *Geelong Advertiser*, 2 May 1846.
45. Christie, op. cit., pp.166-7.

Select Bibliography

The following is a guide to further reading and research into the matters touched on in this book.

Highly Recommended Works

Aborigines in Colonial Victoria 1835-1886, M F Christie, University of NSW Press, Sydney, 1979. This book is unrivalled in its careful documentation and analysis of Aboriginal-European relations in early Victoria. Its bibliography gives excellent guidance for those wishing to pursue these matters at depth.

The Aboriginal Tasmanians, Lyndall Ryan, University of Queensland Press, St Lucia, 1981. This is an invaluable study that does for Tasmanian history what Christie did for Victoria. However, it is wider in its scope, proceeding from pre-white days to take the history of Tasmanian Aborigines right up to recent times.

What Did Happen to the Aborigines of Victoria?, Vol.1, *The Kurnal of Gippsland*, Philip Pepper with Tess De Araugo, Hyland House, Melbourne, 1985. This very recent, well-illustrated and researched book is of great significance in being one of the first Aboriginal histories of Victoria, Philip Pepper being a well-known Victorian Aborigine. It covers from early days up until modern times.

Useful Works

Trucanini: Queen or Traitor?, Vivienne Rae Ellis, Australian Institute of Aboriginal Studies, 1981. This is an account of Truganini's life. *Trucanini* (an alternative spelling of Truganini prefered by the author as more phonetically correct) contains much useful material but its comments do not always seem to be borne out by the research material. It is particularly controversial and poor in its treatment of the present-day Tasmanian Aborigines for, while it refers to their Aboriginal Information Office in Hobart, it refuses to recognise them as descendents, calling Trucanini the 'last known Tasmanian Aborigine.' Ellis's treatment of this issue needs to be contrasted with Ryan's. Ryan, in her work referred to above, amply documents the survival of the Tasmanian Aboriginal community and its eventual recognition by government authorities.

Historical Records of Victoria, Vol.2A, *The Aborigines of Port Phillip 1835-1839*. Victorian Government Printing Office, 1982. Vol.2B, *Aborigines and Protectors 1838-1839*, Victorian Government Printing Office, 1983. These two particular volumes provide a much-needed assembly of well-chosen, early archival material.

1842: The Public Executions of Melbourne, Ian MacFarlane (comp.), Public Records Office of Victoria, 1984. A slim volume documenting the execution in that year of Aborigines and bushrangers.

When the Wattles Bloom Again: The Life and Times of William Barak, Last Chief of the Yarra Yarra Tribe, Shirley Wiencke, self published, 1984.

The Other Side of the Frontier, Henry Reynolds, History Department, James Cook University, Townsville, 1981. A very interesting and thoughtful analysis of the Aboriginal response to the invasion and settlement of Australia.

Research Facilities

La Trobe Library, La Trobe Street, Melbourne. This library holds full sets of parliamentary papers and many valuable early documents. Of particular relevance is *Niel Black's Journal* and Henry Meyrick's correspondence. Both of these as unpublished manuscripts are held in the Manuscripts Section of the Library.

Public Records Office of Victoria, Laverton, Victoria. This holds a vast collection of correspondence and governmental reports. The Public Records Office has a booklet, *Victorian Aborigines 1835-1901: A Resource Guide to the Holdings of the Public Record Office of Victoria*, that guides the way to some of the most useful material on Victorian Aborigines. However it should be noted that despite the efforts of a very helpful but over-worked staff, some material is inadequately catalogued and sometimes improperly filed, so be prepared to survey widely in related areas to find material.

Mitchell Library, Sydney. As Port Phillip came under New South Wales in early days, many valuable documents relating to Melbourne have found their way to Sydney. In particular, Robinson's reports and William Thomas's journals are held there.

National Library, Canberra. This has a wide range of early documents. It is possible to order photocopies of required documents if they can be identified.

Public Records Office, Colonial Office Files, London. This is the home of many valuable government reports and of correspondence of Australian affairs.

The Bookshelf, 116 Bridge Road, Richmond, Victoria. It is not conventional to list a bookshop as a reference library but I believe many people would find this bookshop one of the most valuable places they could go in order to develop a wider knowledge of Victorian and Australian Aboriginal history and affairs. It has one of the finest collections in Australia of books by or about Australian Aborigines.

Index

Aborigines,
  alcohol and, 15, 41, 43, 55, 102
  banned from Melbourne and vicinity, 44, 45, 46-7, 48, 55
  border wars, 1, 37
  bounty for capture of, 7
  British justice applied to, 7, 17-19, 49, 54, 58, 80-9, 96, 101
  Christianization of, 3, 8, 9, 12
  'civilization' of, 3, 8, 13, 25, 38, 40, 66, 100, 102, 106
  corroborees, 41-2, 43, 47, 95
    Gaggip dance, 42
  crimes by, 13, 17, 22, 31, 47, 57, 83, 88
    rape, 7, 13
    murder, 2, 7, 13, 18, 19, 20, 38, 49, 51, 52, 53, 54, 57, 61-4, 69, 78, 80-1, 82, 83-9, 100-1, 102
    robbery, 2, 5, 37, 38, 63-4, 65, 66, 67, 70, 73-4, 77, 79n
    sheep/cattle/horse stealing, 3, 18, 19, 20, 25, 27, 30, 49, 71, 73, 83n, 101, 102, 103, 104-5
  death and burial, 98-9
    demand for skeletons/skulls, 92, 97-8, 99
    desecration of graves, 98
    skulls used as warning by whites, 41
  education for, 14, 105-6
  evolution theory applied to, 92, 97-8
  firearms used by against own people, 51-3, 54, 55, 57, 68, 72
  firearms used by whites against, 2, 3, 4, 7, 9, 17, 25-6, 27, 28, 30, 31, 38, 41, 59, 65, 67-8, 69, 70, 71, 73, 76-7, 101, 102, 103, 104-5
  firearms used in resistance by, 1-2, 3, 6, 19, 46, 48, 51, 56, 57, 61-3, 64, 65, 66, 67, 70, 74, 77, 100
  genocide, 13, 43, 82, 106
  guerrilla warfare by, 8, 102, 105
  health of, 5, 6, 8, 9, 11, 13, 14, 43-4, 97
    influenza epidemics, 6, 39, 43
    smallpox epidemics, 15-16
    venereal diseases, 16, 31, 43
  hunting and food-gathering, 3-4, 16, 25, 26-7, 42, 43, 46, 47, 48, 53, 56, 67, 70, 75, 81, 98
  land rights, 12, 14-15, 81, 82, 95-6, 106-7
  languages, 8, 35, 44, 88
  laws, 81, 88
  marriage 'strategy' for, 5-6, 97 martial law applied to, 2, 7
  massacres of, 3, 4, 6, 7, 12, 17, 18-19, 21, 25, 26, 28, 30-1, 34, 35, 41, 42, 49, 50, 51, 52, 60, 73, 88, 100-1, 102, 103, 104-5
  as mercenaries, 51-3, 54, 72
  missionaries and, 12, 16
  as pacificators of own people, 10-11, 12-13, 14, 38, 66
  poisoning of, 19, 39, 40, 42, 103
  as police, 51, 53, 102-3
  police/troopers used to suppress, 2, 7, 10, 18, 20, 46, 48, 49, 51, 52, 53, 56, 57-8, 61, 63-71, 72-9, 83, 85, 102-3
  protection policy for, 12, 14, 21, 25, 26, 39-41, 45-6, 49-50, 55, 88, 100, 102
  punishment for crimes against own people, 80-1, 87
  punishment for crimes against whites, 2-5, 38, 49, 57-8, 82-3, 84, 87-9, 90-4, 96, 100, 101
  punishment of whites for crimes against, 7, 17-19, 21, 30-1, 42, 49-50, 53, 54, 81-2, 88, 90, 100, 101, 104
  rations for, 12, 14, 40, 42, 44, 45, 46, 48, 55, 96, 102
  reserves/settlements/stations for, 7, 8, 9, 10, 11, 12, 14-15, 39, 44, 46, 47, 55, 60, 8, 96-7, 98, 99, 105, 106-7
  resistance to invasion by, 1-2, 3, 6, 8, 9, 13, 15, 18, 19-20, 21, 25, 33, 34, 36, 46, 47, 48, 55, 56-7, 58, 59-60, 61-79, 84, 86, 88, 99-101, 102, 103, 105, 107
  sealers and, 3, 4, 5, 6, 7, 17, 34, 86, 96, 9, 98
  seizure of tribal lands of, 4, 5, 6, 11-12, 18, 20, 21, 23, 24-5, 26, 27, 28-9, 43, 46, 47-8, 55, 60, 61, 81, 82, 96, 101
  as servants, 2, 14
  settlers and, 1-2, 5, 12, 13, 15, 17, 20, 21, 23, 24-31, 34-5, 38, 42, 44, 46, 47, 48, 49, 50, 51, 55, 59, 60, 61-4, 66, 71, 72-3, 74, 80, 81-2, 97, 99-103, 104-5
  shelters, 3, 16, 29-30, 34, 40, 42
  shepherds and, 3, 4, 5, 19, 21, 30, 49-50, 57, 59
  as slaves, 4, 6, 7, 96, 107
  as trackers, 51, 65, 66, 67, 68, 70-2, 73, 78, 102
  treaties with, 12, 80, 81
  tribal warfare, 41-2, 43, 57
    tournaments, 32
  whalers and, 17, 61-4, 69, 78, 84, 85, 88
  women, 3, 4, 6-7, 16, 17, 18, 26, 27, 32, 52, 54, 57, 58, 59, 60, 66, 77, 82, 85, 86, 95, 96-7, 101, 102, 104
    abduction of, 3, 4, 6, 7
    cohabitation with whites, 7, 8, 16, 3, 43
    as workers for whites, 2, 8, 11, 34, 40, 4, 45, 52, 59, 86, 95-6

Index 119

see *also* Tasmanian Aborigines; Victorian Aborigines
Allan, Mr — (of Dandenong), 66
Allen, Mr (of Westernport), 2, 38, 67, 73
Anderson, Mr (of Westernport), 38, 56, 63, 64, 69, 70, 71, 73-8
Anderson (station-hand for Niel Black), 28
Andersons Inlet, 35n
Arthur, Mary Ann, 95, 96, 98
Arthur, Walter George, 59, 95, 96
Arthurs River, 86
Arthurs Seat, 44, 45, 72
Australian Alps, 42, 104
Ayse, Mr — (of Dandenong), 66

Bacchus, William Henry, 86
Bald Hill, 35n
Barak, 106, 107
Barry, Sir Redmond, 83-5
Barwon River, 20
Bass River, 63
Bass Strait Islands, 99, 107
Batman, John, 10, 16, 95n
Batmans Hill, 17
Beedon, Lucy, 98
Ben Lomond, 3, 6
Benalla, 18
Betty, 99
Big River tribe, 8
Billibellary, 48
Black, Donald, 27, 29-30
Black, Niel, 21-33
Black Line, 8
Blacking, — (overseer for Niel Black), 26
Board for the Protection of Aborigines, 105
Bolden, George, 56, 81-2
Bolin lagoons (Bulleen Ponds), 47, 48
Boneurong dialect, 35n
Boniong, 34, 35
Bonjon, 80-1, 87
Bunurong (Bunnerong) tribe, 16, 35n
  language of, 35
Botany Bay, 16
Bourke, Sir Richard, 17
Bowerman's (Henry) station, 49
Bradley, William, 16
British Anti-Slavery Society, 12, 21
Broken River, 40
Brune, Davy, 7
Brune, Peter, 7, 91, 95
Bruny Island, 6, 7, 8
Bruthen Creek, 102
Buckley, William, 17, 34
Bulleen Ponds (Bolin lagoons), 47
bushrangers, 100
Byng, Mr — (publican), 92

Cape Barren Island, 92
Cape Grim, 3, 4, 6
Cape Patterson, 63, 66
  coal-mine, 61-2, 72
Cape Portland, 7, 99
Cape Schanck, 45, 72
Carrum Swamps, 34
Charlotte, 59
Circular Head (Tas), 4
Clerke, Dr Jonathan, 19
Cockatoo Island, 89
Codd, Clement, 101
Codd, Patrick, 100-1
Colac, 51
Collins, Lt-Col David, 17
Colourt Station, 2, 34-5, 36, 38, 73
Cook, William, 62, 63
Corranderrk Reserve, 106, 107
Count Alpha, *see* Woorraddy
Cox, John, 101
Cranbourne, 64
Crowther, Dr William, 98
Cussen, Dr Patrick, 43

Dana, Henry Edward Pulteney, 102
Dandenong, 1-2, 63-4, 66, 72, 100, 102
Davies, John (Public Executioner), 92, 93, 94
D'Entrecasteaux Channel, 6, 98, 99
Derwent River, 6
Devils River, 42
Dray, 7
Dredge, James, 40, 41, 49, 93

Ellis, John (bushranger), 100
Emu Bay, 6
Evans, Samuel, 62, 84

Fairfield Infectious Diseases Hospital, 47
Fairlea Women's Prison, 47
Faithfull, William Pitt, 18, 19
Fanny (Planobeena), 3, 6, 9, 59, 107
  armed resistance by, 1-2, 60, 61-4, 65, 66, 67, 68, 71, 72, 73-4
  hunt for and capture of, 65-79
  return to Flinders Island, 95-6
  trial of, 83-9
Fawkner, John Pascoe, 17
Fitzroy, 37
Flemington, 37
Flinders Island Aboriginal settlement, 8, 9, 96, 98, 107
  closure of, 96-7
  petition to Queen Victoria from, 96
  removal to Port Phillip, 10-11, 13-14, 39-40
  return from Port Philip, 59, 95-7

Fogarty, 'Young' (bushranger), 100
Foster, Mr —, 70
Framlingham, 106, 107
Franklin, Sir John, 13-14
Franklin, Johnny, 95
Frankston, 44
Fraser, Major — (of Mornington Peninsula), 36
Fraser, Miss —, 36

Gaggip dance, 42
Gardiner, John, 19
Gardiner Reservoir, 35n
Geelong, 20, 48, 51-2, 54, 66
    tribes, 16, 20, 48, 49
Geelong Advertiser cited, 105-6
Gipps, Sir George, 13-14, 19-20, 30, 44, 57, 66, 80, 82, 88, 101, 104
    Aboriginal rations reduced by, 40, 55
    firearms ban by, 48, 53, 57
    on Aboriginal rights, 87
Gippsland, 33, 74, 100, 102, 104, 107
    tribes, 100, 102, 104
Gisborne, Henry Fyshe, 56
Glenelg, Baron Charles Grant, 9, 11, 14, 19, 20, 40, 44
Glenormiston (Strathdownie) Station, 26
Goulburn River, 19, 41, 49
    tribes, 19, 35, 47, 49, 57, 58, 106, 107
Grampians, 37, 102
Grange River, 100
Gurmai tribe, 35n

Hamilton's (William) Station, 49
Healesville, 47, 106
Hawdon, Joseph, 71
Heidelberg, 48
Henty, James, 54
Hill, Mr — (from Sydney), 42
Hind, Mr — (of Westernport), 38
Hobson, Edward, 44, 69, 70
Hopkins River, 82
Horsefal (?Hosfold), Mr — (of Dandenong), 64
Hume Highway, 20
Hurst, Rev Benjamin, 50

Indented Head, 51
Inman, Walter, 61, 63
Isaac, 59, 60

Jack of Cape Grim (Tunnerminnerwait), 3-5, 6, 8-9, 107
    armed resistance by, 1-2, 60, 61-4, 65, 66, 67, 68, 71, 72, 73-4, 78
    execution of, 90-4, 102
    hunt for and capture of, 65-79
    named Napoleon by Robinson, 9
    rebellion advocated by, 60
    trial of, 83-9
Jackie Jackie, 56
Jackson, Samuel, 19
Jacoort tribe, 26
Jaga Jaga, 16
    tribe, 15
Jamieson, Robert, 63, 71
Jeanneret, Charles, 95-7
Jennings, Corporal —, 73
Jepps, Vandie, 100
Jika Jika,
    wife of, 54
Jimmerson, Mr — (of Cape Schanck), 45
Jin Jin, 18
Johnson, Corporal William, 63, 78
Jones, Thomas, 20
Jubilee History of Victoria cited, 102
Julian Range, 49

Kangaroo Island, 4, 99
Kannang (Yallock Creek), 61
Kelly, Patrick, 83
Kirkland, Mrs Katherine, 27
Koroite Station, 103
Kulin Confederation, 106 language group, 35n

Ladys Bay, 62
Lake Colac, 52
Lake Condah, 102, 106, 107
Lake Corangamite, 50, 107
Lalla Rookh, see Truganini
Langhorne, Alfred, 59, 86
Langhorne, George, 16-17
Langhorne, Mr (Aboriginal tracker), 68
Lanney, William, 98
La Trobe, Charles Joseph, 31, 40, 47, 50, 54-5, 56, 57, 58, 59, 61, 63, 66, 70, 73, 76, 88, 89, 95, 101, 102
    expulsion of Aborigines from Melbourne, 44, 46-7, 55, 82
    on Aboriginal rights, 82
    refusal to arm Aboriginal trackers, 72
Launceston, 97
Leighton Station, 82
Lettsom, Major Samuel, 57-8
Lively, Mr (Aboriginal tracker), 68
Loddon River, 41
Lonsdale, Capt William, 17, 44, 52, 53, 54
lyre-birds (bullen-bullen),
    trade in tails, 46, 53, 54

Macalister, Lachlan, 100
Macalister River, 100, 104
McArthur, Donald Gordon, 54

Mackay's Station, 57
McNicol, Donald, 29
Macquarie Harbour, 3, 4
Manimet tribe, 52
Maoris of New Zealand, 81, 97
Mary Anne, see Arthur, Mary Ann
Massie, Mr — (of Westernport), 56, 61, 62, 63
Matilda (Pyterrunner), 3, 5, 8-9, 59, 107
    armed resistance by, 1-2, 60, 61-4, 65, 66, 67, 68, 71, 72, 73-4
    hunt for and capture of, 65-79
    return to Flinders Island, 95-6
    trial of, 83-9
Melbourne, 20, 37, 39, 41, 45, 57, 66, 73, 79
    attitude of settlers to Aborigines, 43, 46, 55
    beginnings of settlement, 1, 2, 16, 17, 22, 34
    descriptions of, 17, 22, 24, 31-2, 33, 34, 36, 37
    expulsion of Aborigines from, 44, 45, 46-7, 48, 55
    land values, 34, 47-8
    population of, 1, 23, 34
    public executions in, 90-4, 100, 101, 104
Melbourne Cemetery (old,
    Aboriginal graveyard outside, 94
Melbourne Gaol (New), 37, 92
Melbourne Gaol (Old), 37, 90, 91
Mercer, Mr —, 77
Merri Creek, 47
    Aboriginal school at junction of Yarra and, 105-6
Merrick, Mr — (of Mornington Peninsula), 44
Meyrick, Henry, 2, 21, 33-8, 44, 73, 100, 102, 103-5
Meyrick, Maurice, 33, 34, 104
mirr-n'yong root, 26-7
Mornington Peninsula, 2, 17, 33, 34, 36, 37-8, 44-5, 46, 52, 56, 59, 73, 102
    tribes, 34, 36, 102
Mount Eliza, 35
Mount Gambier, 103
Mount Macedon, 49, 53
Mount Martha, 56
Mount Napier, 102
Mount Piper, 49
Mount Rouse, 101, 102
Mundy, Mr — (of Dandenong), 1, 49, 64, 66, 71, 79
Murray River, 86, 103, 106
Murrumbidgee River, 52, 54
Muston Creek, 101
Myall Creek massacre, 18-19, 21, 42, 88

Napoleon, see Jack of Cape Grim
Narren Guillen Station, 35-6

Native Police Corps, 51, 53, 102-3
Nerruknerbook, 57-8
New South Wales Legislative Council,
    Committee inquiry into Aborigines, 13
Northcote, 48

Old Settlement Hill, 71
Ordon, Mr — (of Dandenong), 64
Orton, Rev Joseph, 41-2, 91
Otway Ranges, 26
Ovens River, 19, 20, 40
Oyster Cove, 97-8, 99
    Aboriginal cemetery at, 98

Pagerly, 7
Pakenham, 63
Parker, Edward Stone, 40, 41, 49, 51-2, 58
Patrick — (whaler), 62
Peevay, see Smallboy, Robert
Phillip Island, 63
Pigeon (Aboriginal tracker), 68
Planobeena, see Fanny
Plenty River, 99, 100
Plunkett, John Hubert, 49-50
Point Nepean, 33, 55, 59
Police, native,
    see Native Police Corps
Port Arthur, 86
Port Davey, 99
Port Fairy, 102
Port Phillip,
    immigration to, 23, 36-7, 38, 55, 103
    population of, 38
    settlement of, 20, 23-4, 103
Port Phillip Advertiser cited, 100
Port Phillip Debating Society, 100
Port Phillip Gazette cited, 88-9, 90, 93, 100, 103
Port Phillip Herald cited, 1, 37, 66, 70, 73-4, 76, 78, 85, 86, 88, 92, 99
Port Phillip Patriot cited, 57, 58, 90, 103
Port Pirie, 5
Portland, 10, 17, 26, 28, 30, 35
Portland Mercury cited, 102
Powlett, Frederick Armand, 2, 29, 61, 63, 64-71, 72, 73-9
    at trial, 84, 85
Powlett River, 63, 75
Purbrick, W. J., 103
Pyterrunner, see Matilda

Rawson, Lieut Samuel, 61, 63, 64-71, 72, 7
Riddle, Mr —, 24
Robbins Island, 3
Robert, see Smallboy, Robert
Robins, Robert, 85-6

Robinson, George Augustus, 16, 19, 26, 60, 91, 92, 94, 100
   administration of Port Phillip Protectorate, 39-40, 41, 42-4, 45-6, 47-8, 51-2, 54-5, 57, 59, 66, 71-2
   appointed Chief Protector of Aborigines, 12, 14
   custody of Tasmanian women after trial, 88, 95
   evidence at trial of Tasmanians, 86-7, 98
   life saved by Truganini, 8, 86
   matrimonial strategy advocated by, 5-6
   relationship with Truganini, 8
   relieved of responsibility for Tasmanians, 59, 95
   removal of Tasmanians to Port Phillip, 2, 3, 5, 10-15, 18, 38
   round-up of Tasmanian Aborigines, 4-6, 7-9, 97
Roger the Russian (Aborigine), 100, 101
Royal College of Surgeons, London, 98
Royal Melbourne Institute of Technology, 92
Royal Society of Tasmania, 98
Rusden, H. K., 97
Russell, Lieut F. B., 63
Ryrie's Station, 56

St Kilda, 35n
Sandy Point, 2, 34
Scots Church, Melbourne, 37
sealers, 3, 4, 5, 6, 7, 17, 34, 86, 96, 97, 98
Settlement Point, 64
shepherds, 3, 4, 5, 19, 21, 22, 24, 25, 30, 49-50, 59
Sievwright, Charles Wightman, 25, 26, 27, 28, 30-1, 40, 41, 43, 49-50, 82
Smallboy, Robert (Peevay), 3, 6, 7, 8-9, 59, 107
   armed resistance by, 1-2, 60, 61-4, 65, 66, 67, 71, 72, 73-4, 78
   execution of, 90-4, 102
   hunt for and capture of, 83-9
   trial of, 83-9
Smith and Osbrey's Station, 101
Snodgrass, Peter, 47
Society of Friends (Quakers),
   purchase of land from North American Indians, 81
South Australia, 22, 59
South Yarra, 18
Stanley, Lord Edward, 57, 101
Stephen, James, 13, 96
Stokell, Dr G., 98
Strathdownie (Glenormiston) Station, 26
Suke, 99
Supreme Court, Melbourne, 15, 18, 80

Surrey Hills, 3
Sydney, 11, 16, 18, 19, 20, 21-2, 33, 34, 37, 39, 40, 42, 57, 81

Takier, 81-2
Tamar River Valley, 3, 6
Tarerenorerer (Walyer), 6
Tarwin River, 75
Tasmania,
   land values, 11-12, 96
Tasmanian Aborigines,
   Big River Tribe, 8
   good 'labourers', 11
   'last' of, 97, 98, 99, 106
   North-West Tribe, 3-4
   removal to Port Phillip, 3, 5, 10-14, 18, 39, 59, 84
   resistance to invasion, 2, 6, 8, 9, 79n, 84
   return from Port Phillip, 95-6, 98
   'round-up' of, 3, 4-9, 11, 12, 60, 97, 98
   South-East Tribe, 3, 6
   South-West Tribe, 3-4
Tasmanian Land Company, 4
Taungurong, 106
Taylor, Frederick, 26, 28
Tench, Watkin, 16
Thomas, Mrs Susannah, 46
Thomas, William, 19, 39, 64
   appointed Assistant Protector of Aborigines, 40
   as Protector of Westernport district, 41, 44-6, 47-8, 51, 52-4, 55-6, 57-8, 59, 60, 86, 100, 103
   as Protector of Yarra Bank encampments, 41, 42-3, 44
   hunt for Tasmanians by, 2, 66-72, 73-9, 89
   lost in bush on Mornington Peninsula, 45, 52
Thomas, William, Jnr, 60
Thompson River, 105
Thompson, Rev Adam, 91, 93, 94
Thongworong tribe, 49
Timmy, 59
Tobinnerk, 71
Truganini (Trucannini), 3, 6-7, 59, 107
   armed resistance by, 1-2, 60, 61-4, 65, 66, 67, 68, 71, 72, 73-4, 78
   assistance given to Robinson by, 6, 8-9, 13, 97
   death and burial of, 98-9
   hunt for and capture of, 65-79
   'marriage' of, 97
   named Lalla Rookh by Robinson, 9
   relationship with Robinson, 8
   return to Flinders Island, 95-7
   Robinson's life saved by, 8, 86
   trial of, 83-9

Index 123

Tullamarine, 18
Tunnerminnerwait, see Jack of Cape Grim

Umarrah, 8
Unwin, Frederick, 48

Van Diemen's Land, see Tasmania
Venus Bay, 75
Victoria, Qeen
   150th Anniversary, 107
Victoria, Queen,
   Flinders Island Aborigines' petition to, 96
Victoria Market, 94
Victoria, 150th Anniversary
Victorian Aborigines,
   Bonurong (Bunnerong) tribe, 16, 35, 42
   Gurmai tribe, 35n
   Jacoort tribe, 26
   Kulin Confederation, 35n, 106
   Manimet tribe, 52
   resistance to invasion, 2, 13, 15, 18, 19, 20, 21, 25, 26, 34, 36, 38, 46, 47, 48, 55, 56-7, 58, 60, 99-101, 102, 103, 105
   Watowrong tribe, 16
   Waworong tribe, 16, 39
   Wurundjeri tribe, 47, 48, 106
   see also Geelong tribes, Gippsland tribes, Goulburn River tribes, Mornington Peninsula tribes, Westernport tribes, Yarra River tribes
Victory Hill, 3, 4
Vignolles, — (military officer), 72

Walter, see Arthur, Walker
Walyer, see Tarerenorerer
Wannon River, 103
Warrandyte, 56
Warrnambool, 107
Watowrong tribe, 16
Watson, Mr — (coal-mine overseer, Cape Patterson), 61, 62, 63, 85-6
Waworong tribe, 16, 39
Wedge, John Helder, 17, 101
Wedge's Station, 100-1
Wentworth, Charles, 83
Westaway, Mr — (of Dandenong), 2, 65, 66, 72, 73
Western District, 82, 102, 107
Westernport, 1, 2, 21, 34-5, 36, 38, 41, 55, 56, 57, 59, 60, 61-79, 86, 104
   tribes, 16, 17, 34-5
whalers, 17, 61-4, 69, 78, 84, 85, 88
White brothers (of Portland Bay), 30-1
Willis, Judge John Walpole, 15, 80-2, 83, 84, 87, 88, 92, 95, 101, 105
Wilsons Promontory, 17, 35n

Windberry, 57
Winnaberrie, 47
Wonga, 106
Woolnorth, 96
Woorraddy (Count Alpha), 7, 9, 59
Wurundgeree dialect, 35n
Wurundjeri tribe, 47, 48, 106

Yallock Creek (Kannang), 61
'Yankee' (whaler), 62, 63, 78, 85, 86
Yarra Bend Park, 48
Yarra Glen, 56
Yarra River, 38, 105
   Aboriginal reserve on, 14-15
   native encampments on, 32-3, 39-41, 43-4, 46-8, 55-6, 58, 59, 72, 80,
   tribes, 16, 17, 35n, 46, 47, 48, 51-2, 53, 55-6, 58, 106, 107
Yea, 47
Yaldwyn, William Henry, 20

Jan Roberts

Jan Roberts has worked extensively with Aboriginal groups in Australia and her research into their history since white settlement has led her to write *The Mapoon Books*, a study of Aboriginal settlements in North Queensland, and *Massacres to Mining*. Of this latter book Xavier Herbert said it is 'a work deserving to be a classic in our history!'

Jan also works as a freelance investigative journalist and has worked in film and television, producing an edited version of *Ningla-A-Na*, a documentary on Aboriginal issues, and she initiated, co-produced and directed *Munda Nyuringi* which gives the story of the last great Australian goldrush – as seen by the Aborigines who survived it. This documentary was nominated for the AFI Awards in 1985.

Jan is now working on the production of *Jack of Cape Grim* as a major television mini-series.

www.ingramcontent.com/pod-product-compliance
Ingram Content Group UK Ltd.
Pitfield, Milton Keynes, MK11 3LW, UK
UKHW041428180426
11947UKWH00007B/340

9 780955 917707